T0209851

CREDIBILITY MATTERS

LEARN IT. LIVE IT. LEAD IT!

MARTIN KUSCUS

WestBow Press books may be ordered through booksellers or by contacting:

WestBow Press
A Division of Thomas Nelson & Zondervan
1663 Liberty Drive
Bloomington, IN 47403
www.westbowpress.com
844-714-3454

ISBN: 978-1-6642-4092-6 (sc)
ISBN: 978-1-6642-4145-9 (hc)
ISBN: 978-1-6642-4144-2 (e)

Library of Congress Control Number: 2021915054

Print information available on the last page.

WestBow Press rev. date: 09/08/2021

WHAT OTHERS ARE SAYING ABOUT THIS BOOK....

"It has been a great pleasure for me to have known Martin Kuscus for many years and throughout this time I have recognized the leadership positions he has held, which he handled with the utmost integrity resulting in great success. I have also had the privilege of reading his new book entitled *Credibility Matters*. This book captures the essence of leadership. It communicates the crises we are facing due to a lack of leadership, showing us how those at the helm have let us down and disappointed the people they served, particularly in our own country. Most importantly, Martin's book captures the glaring need for credible and ethical leadership in our society. Let me dare say globally as well. It will help the up-coming generation to avoid the pitfalls of leadership by learning from the mistakes of others.

I really encourage everyone to read this book - you will gain great insight from it and sharpen your leadership skills."

Enjoy the book!

Pastor Ray McCauley
Senior Pastor Rhema Bible Church North – South Africa
President - International Fellowship of Christian Churches (IFCC)

"My first meeting with Martin Kuscus left a very deep impression on me. I had just joined Old Mutual and was taken by one of my colleagues, to meet someone she described as "a wonderful man" who was both CEO of the South African Bureau of Standards and Chairman of the Government Employee Pension Fund. I couldn't quite understand how someone could combine a demanding day job as a CEO of one critical national institution with moonlighting as Chair of one of the largest retirement funds in the world! I met a man who wore his position lightly, his convictions deeply and exuded a warm, deeply affecting humanity. Some years later, when I was at Liberty and we were looking for a Chairperson for the Synergy Income Fund, I had no hesitation recommending Martin to my colleagues. I had by then come to know him as a man of great depth, resolution, wisdom and integrity. I know of no one more qualified to speak on credibility and character in addressing one of the greatest needs of our age – credible, inclusive, authentic leadership that delivers for everyone. There is much food for thought and much more that will delight the soul. I urge you to come and dine."

Samuel Ogbu
Group Chief Executive Officer – Old Mutual West Africa.

"I had the privilege of growing up in the same township as Martin Kuscus and his book brought a flood of memories of our childhood and journey together. This book is so relevant for our times because it captures the rich and painful history of the South African tapestry and brings the reader to homegrown truths that will inspire, instruct and revitalize. Martin speaks about a leadership that is present, not loud and charismatic but a stabilizing force in the midst of chaos, confusion and upheaval. Enjoy the journey through the many stories of real people that chose a life of credibility."

Dr Serge Solomons *(MD)*

"In a world where the leadership light seems to be getting dimmer and dimmer, I'm glad that we still have amongst us shining examples to help us light the way so that we may better navigate the leadership journey. I've known Martin Kuscus for many years and what I can tell you about him is that integrity is integral to who he is. His life story and leadership journey, so magnificently captured in this book testify of the importance of faith, vision and the willingness to put your hands where your heart is. It is said that there are no short-cuts to success and as you read this book, you will discover that no matter how hard the road may seem, God has a way of making a way even where there seems to be no way. Thank you Mr Kuscus, for putting your thoughts and beliefs on paper. You have enriched not only this generation, but the generations to follow as well. May you keep shining your leadership light."

Prof Maurice Radebe
Director of Wits Business School
Chairman of Unleashing Leadership Potential

"*Credibility Matters* is a must-read by all newcomers and veteran leaders. Martin has reached deep within himself, drawing from his wealth of knowledge and experience as a leader and mentor; sharing the greatest tools he used to become a leader of note. His captivating, transparent, truthful and unashamedly twisted leadership journey, will undoubtedly assist and correct leaders towards credibility without compromise. I pray that the Lord will open your hearts to receiving this blessing from Martin and share his journey with many more leaders worldwide, so we can build credible leaders especially now with all the challenges we are facing in society!"

Dr Snowy Khoza
Chief Executive Officer: Bigen Africa.

"Martin Kuscus and I have been on a journey together to live and lead well. As I interact with leaders worldwide, there are few who rival Martin's insights on leadership and relationships. It is so refreshing to know an author who personally reflects what he writes. My hope for global leaders is that this book will impact them as Martin has impacted me."

Steven French
L^x Partners, Founder
Lifework Leadership, Global Ambassador

"Martin Kuscus' book on his life and leadership journey is a must-read by all leaders and those aspiring leadership positions alike. How he narrated his rise from obscurity to the commanding heights of power and influence will certainly liberate many people and clarify the myth of whether leaders are born or made. Martin managed to capture such wealth of leadership experiences gain over many years in a single book. Coming from such a humble background, he managed to prove that '*our past, no matter how bad or good it was, does not define our future*'. People of every nation and tribe, whether in corporate, religious or public sector, the world-over, can learn and apply true servanthood, ethical and credible leadership principles that Martin so intelligibly penned down."

Professor Watson Ladzani
University of South Africa

"I was approached by Martin after his retirement from politics and his next big move into the corporate life, to coach him through his "Half Time". Half Time is a period between the first half of your life and the second half where you "go into the locker room and make eye contact with God to get your assignment from Him for the second half or next season". What I appreciated most of our journey together, was Martin's humility and vulnerability and above all his utmost desire to seek God's will for His life. One of Martin's missions is to serve upcoming leaders with his wealth of experience and wisdom. I believe this book will contribute to an eternal legacy for many upcoming leaders who desire to serve well."

Mathilda Fourie
International HalfTime Coach
HalfTime Institute

"Idolization, power-mongering and manipulation have become all too commonplace in society and our institutions. This game needs to come to an end! With more than 60,000 leadership books available on Amazon, why do we still have a crisis with leadership today? Most of these books are useful enablers but what cannot be overemphasized is that leadership is primarily a matter of the heart. *Credibility Matters* changes the leadership conversation by challenging us to look beyond charisma while embracing character as an absolute essential for today's leader. Martin applies decades of practical experience, wisdom, and whit as he takes the reader on a journey examining the motivation, intentions, and authenticity of leaders. Pointing to Jesus as the archetype of servant leadership, this book is a must-read for anyone pursuing significance as a leader."

Rich Cummins
President/CEO - Lead Like Jesus

"If anybody ever ask me whether I can vouch for Martin Kuscus, my answer will undoubtedly be: YES! I can and I will vouch for this man. When Martin asked me to read through his book, I could not put it down. I heard Martin speak on several occasions and I followed his life and he is who he says he is. As a white Afrikaner woman growing up in a privileged home, my ears had filters and my eyes had blinkers on. In a way I think I was ignorant to the reality of the world around me. Reality is, I read Martin's book and I can never claim ignorance again. Because I once was blind, but now I see. Martin is a man of absolute integrity and I know that the authenticity in which he shared his story and related hard earned lessons, can be the pitstops that many people desperately need to stop by and decide to learn, unlearn and relearn. This book will transform your heart and your mind and it has the power in it to make you a co-labourer of bringing about the systemic change our world needs. The system surely is broken, and with this book, Martin is providing evidence that we can be the difference if we choose to be credible people who are called for a time such as this. I vouch for this man, and for this great work he has done."

Christa de Wet
General Manager – Organisational Development, AFGRI

"This book *Credibility Matters*, comes at a very opportune time, when there are serious leadership challenges - corruption, unscrupulous practices and impunity across the private and public sectors of our country. The book raises relevant and profound issues of leadership and the values necessary to excel in this regard. The book is also an inspiration to young people of all walks of life on how a nurse from Tshepong Hospital and raised in humble circumstances in Alabama township, could rise to become a MEC of Finance, CEO of SABS, Chairman of the Government Employee Pension Fund, director of numerous JSE listed companies and a businessman. The book documents a life well-lived by Martin Kuscus who did not only discharge his responsibilities with excellence but has also done so with high levels of integrity.

I have known Martin for over two decades and have benefited immensely from his mentorship and friendship. I am particularly proud of his achievements over the years both in his public and private life. South Africa and the world are crying out for leaders of his calibre and character."

Malungelo Zilimbola
Founder and CEO of Mazi Asset Management

Dedication

This book is dedicated to all the frontline healthcare workers throughout the world who gallantly led the battle against the Covid-19 pandemic from the front. Your unselfish care, compassion and courage in the midst of unrelenting waves of the pandemic, was a monumental statement of credibility. We especially salute those who paid the supreme price; your sacrifices will forever be etched in our memories.

Contents

Foreword

I am indeed thankful for the opportunity to write this Foreword for *Credibility Matters* by Martin Kuscus. Martin and I have worked together in conferences throughout South Africa over the years. I have always appreciated his unique depth of thought, arresting clarity and insight, rare business acumen, and distinctive spiritual wisdom combined in an engaging delivery style. He has always left me and audiences wanting more after his presentations.

After reading the manuscript, I believe that every person in our culture, particularly those in a leadership position, would benefit immensely from reading this book because as Martin documents and clearly explains, we are in a leadership crisis. All over the globe, in every institution that matters, church, government, corporate, NGO's, etc., surveys reflect a serious lack of trust. I am not sure in human history that we have had such a global crisis in confidence and credibility of leadership as we experience today. The implications of such a lack of credibility are devastating to the human family. Let me suggest and offer support to the arguments put forward, by relaying my sense of a few of the devastating effects.

I once had a mentor, a Jewish Rabbi Edwin H. Friedman, who taught me so many valuable lessons about leadership. When I read *Credibility Matters*, I could not help but reflect upon the leadership principles that Friedman taught, two specifically that come to mind and again add to and support the many reflections in these pages. Firstly, Friedman taught that we could discuss leadership by analogy as a rare and precious commodity, like gold, diamonds, air, water, or forests. Let us think through this analogy for a moment by looking briefly at a precious commodity like forests.

Most scientists agree that if human beings would slow the pace of climate change, preserve precious wildlife, and support the needs of billions of people on planet earth, that trees are a critical part of the solution. Yet, on a daily basis the mass destruction of trees continues oblivious to the dire warnings of conservationists and scientists. Forests cover about 30 per cent of the world land area. Between 1990 and 2016 the world lost 502,000 square miles or 1.3 million square kilometres of forest, an area larger than South Africa. Trees absorb the carbon dioxide human beings exhale and the heat-trapping greenhouse gases that human activity emit. These gases, when entering the atmosphere, increases global warming, what we know as climate change. Given this reality, we as the human family run headlong into the abyss.

In my mind, the crisis of global warming is hitting us and will hit us even more because the precious resource of leadership is sorely lacking. A lack of leadership contributes and accelerates the diminishing of limited resources and leads to destruction. Martin's book must be read based on needing to learn how to be good stewards of leadership; how to preserve leadership; how to take care of it; how to value it. The question is how can we be good stewards of leadership? How do we preserve it?

Secondly, a lack of leadership is so devastating because, as Friedman taught, leadership is like the immune system in the body that guards against and protects against germs, pathogens, and viruses and preserves the health and balance in the body. The human body has germs, pathogens, and potential diseases floating through it all the time. The body is never disease and germ free, but the immune system functions to keep the diseases, germs, and pathogens in check. The immune system of the body preserves a precious balance that allows the germs and diseases to exist in the body, but not function as such that they overwhelm the body and we suffer from illness and disease. When disease occurs, it is not the presence of germs and viruses that cause it, but their replication. The replication of germs and viruses overwhelms the immune system and compromises the body's ability to function. The immune system can no longer preserve the proper balance, so damage occurs and sometimes death. The question then becomes, how does society and its institutions maintain the same kind of balance that occurs in a healthy body? How do we stimulate the immune system?

Credible leadership is the immune system in the church, government, corporate world, NGO's etc. When leadership is not credible, society's immune system is compromised; "germs" and "pathogens" replicate and the body become sick. The germs and pathogens in my country, for instance, are the conspiracy theorists, people that will put party over the country, leaders who deny truth and vote to support lies and deceit, such as Donald J. Trump won the election. Viruses believe that one race, ideology, or party should dominate others regardless of the means to gain and retain dominance and power. Viruses do not care about credibility. They do not care about the long-term health of the body; they only care about their replication in pursuit of its continued existence, power, and control.

I believe that we overemphasize the power of viruses. Viruses replicate because that is what viruses do – that is their life principle, even if they end up killing their host and they themselves die in the process. Rather than focus on society's viruses, what about the response of the immune system? What stimulates the immune system? What makes the immune system stronger to keep the viruses in check? How do we preserve and strengthen the immune system? I am more concerned that people who represent the immune system should read the book than viruses. There is no sense in persuading viruses, their life principle is merely to replicate to the destruction of everyone and everything else. The good news is that the immune system can and must be boosted and this is the major objective of this book.

I believe that the health of the immune system will determine whether or not we combat global warming, whether the energy needs of the balance of the human family will be met; whether we have enough water in a world that is 75% water; whether liberty, justice, and democracy will be established or perish from the face of the earth. So much of our future will be determined by the credibility of leadership.

I imagine that you bought this book because you wanted to be part of the solution rather than being part of the problem. You want to be an antibody in the immune system rather than a virus. I salute you, so let us read every page together to stimulate our immune response. The health of the human family depends on it.

From one antibody to another.

Frank A. Thomas
Professor of Homiletics
Christian Theological Seminary
Indianapolis, Indiana USA

Introduction

The world is facing a crisis and that is a crisis of credible leadership. Many of our leaders in the broader spectrum of society are no longer trusted, believed or respected. If one browses through the media headlines on any given day, there are just too many instances of trust that has been betrayed, values expediently abandoned, high levels of exploitation and manipulation by immensely powerful people in society.

As the world is currently battling the Covid-19 pandemic, it feels like the pressing of the reset button on all fronts – Governments, the economy, families, healthcare, the world of work, sport, recreation, travel, worship, education and virtually every facet of our lives have been impacted. Regrettably, many in our leadership ranks were shown to have feet cast in iron and clay and were found seriously wanting. Let me clarify that this was not entirely a function of Covid-19, but a progressive deterioration of the credibility among those in our leadership that has been slipping for a while now. The pandemic merely brought it into High-Definition (HD) mode turning the world into a fishbowl for most leaders, with no place to hide. The bar has lately been set so low over the passage of time in which we have sacrificed character for charisma and moral rectitude for popular appeal.

The causative factors that gave rise to this situation include, amongst others:

- Apathy: A total lack of enthusiasm, interest or real concern from the led on whose behalf leaders derive their mandate. We have tolerated mediocre outputs from our leaders and accepted them as the norm.

- Political correctness: It is a situation in which we do not want to upset the applecart and an almost reluctance to challenge the status quo. Some of us have become so beholden to the patronage of leaders that we dare not speak up or interrogate their course of action, no matter how wrong it might be.

Transparency International released the 2020 Global Corruption Perception Index earlier this year. It noted that more than two thirds of the 180 countries analysed, scored below 50%. The authors of the report, in emphasising the extent of the crisis, stated the following: "*Our analysis shows that corruption not only undermines the global health response to Covid-19 but contributes to a continuing crisis of democracy*" [1]Lest we hasten to point a finger at the public sector, given some of the high-profile cases that have made the headlines in the mass media, Transparency International's analysis also came to the conclusion in its Trouble at the Top series, that the problem of leadership was just as serious in the private sector as they were in the public sector. Over the last several years, multi-national companies based in "clean" or seemingly corruption-free countries have been implicated in high profile cases of money laundering, foreign bribery and other private sector corruption.[2] They mentioned five cases of corruption in this article that make even the "cleanest" countries look dirty. Notables include Airbus, Semlex, Gunvor, Bombardier and San Faustin.

Here in South Africa, our headlines have been saturated through much of year 2020, with large scale corruption involving Covid-19 Personal Protective Equipment (PPE) and feeding programmes related to government tenders. The horror stories coming out of the Zondo Commission (on State Capture) during the last two years boggle the mind and speak to the very heart of a crisis of leadership in the country's young democracy. Looting of the public purse with impunity from high profile personalities, eroded public trust in our leadership cadres. In the private sector, cases like Steinhoff where R200 billion of the market capitalisation was destroyed in 2017, remain unresolved at the time of publishing this book. And then came the contradiction and irony of self-same Steinhoff offering to sponsor the National Prosecuting Authority to investigate and prosecute on the same matter? Imagine turkeys funding Thanksgiving in the 21st century? Other notables in the private sector who have also been fingered on highly corrupt activities include EOH, McKinsey, VBS Bank and Trillian.

When we consider the socio-economic fibre of our country South Africa; to say that we are in a crisis, would be the understatement of the decade. Economically – we are in the throes of a longer recession. On the political front, kleptocracy and factionalism amongst the ruling elite keeps rising. Socially, we have witnessed the most horrendous incidences of women and child abuse on a scale and intensity previously unheard of in our society. Spiritually, the church faces a credibility crisis where false doctrine is rife and people duped into all manner of theatricals and even fake miracles.

Over the past 35+ years, I had the privilege to serve in various leadership positions at both the public sector and corporate levels, locally and internationally. In many instances I was thrown into the deep end. As I reflected on my leadership journey, I gained a fresh appreciation for it and the valuable lessons learnt. When I began this leadership journey, it was very much a trial- and- error approach. There was no precedent for the new democratic architecture we wanted to construct for South Africa and experience was not as readily available as is now. But one thing was certain, the founding fathers of this new democratic dispensation had the moral credentials and visionary foresight. Their legacy and the example they imparted to us, inspired us to give it our best shot and operate within a context of relational integrity.

One of my passions is leadership development. Someone once said, you must not waste a good crisis. During the pandemic, I had a lot of time to think as all my work transitioned online and I did not have to spend time travelling from my base in Hartbeespoort, North West Province of South Africa to attend to meetings, conduct coaching sessions or other business engagements. Given the prevailing set of circumstances in our leadership ranks, it would, I believe be tragic if I do not share my experiences with a wider audience. By so doing, they can avoid making and/or repeating the mistakes I made earlier; the school fees have already been paid. Hence, I wrote this book out of a genuine and sincere concern for the next generation of leaders. The central message of the book is to challenge and encourage the reader to live life with the highest degree of credibility in a world in which compromise reigns supreme. This book offers practical tools on becoming an authentic, trusted, reliable and respected voice that shapes the thinking, behaviour, and values of your world for the better, in the midst of so many distractions.

Each one of us has a unique story that needs to be respected, appreciated and validated. There is a multiplicity of stories which we carry with us; some good and some perhaps not so good. This book is not intended to capture the entirety of my life thus far. However, I would like to invite you on a journey, where I will share just a few highlights that shaped my thinking, values and behaviour as I grew up and later took on some very serious leadership assignments. I will also share practical examples as well as the lessons I have acquired along the way. The latter is denoted by what I call "Pitstops" in the respective chapters.

Let me assure you the reader, that I will not challenge you on something which I have not applied in my own life yet. It is my conviction that the relevance, practical application, and impact that these lessons had in my own life, will help you shift the dial in your life as well.

Our world is currently not in good shape, and we cannot allow this state of affairs to persist indefinitely. The unprecedented amount of uncertainty and the myriad of related challenges can have a serious bearing on people's lives and livelihoods. We are called upon as leaders to rise to the occasion in our various spheres of influence, to turn the tide around. You cannot correct what you are not willing to confront. I trust that the principles I am advancing in this book, will be digested with enthusiasm and implemented in your life with courage.

PART A – A LEADER LOST AND FOUND

Chapter 1

WHO RAISES THE VILLAGE?

There is an old African proverb that says: "It takes a village to raise a child." I would like to flip this statement with a question: If it takes a village to raise a child, who raises the village?

In a deeply entrenched economic system of globalization and extremely fast levels of connectivity, the world is nowadays commonly referred to as a global village. This then begs the question "Who raises this village?" Who are the voices that shape the thinking, behaviour and value system of our world? Who are those among us whose good judgement, borne out of hard - earned experience, can be trusted as we grapple with the vexing developmental challenges in our village moving forward? Who are the custodians of the ethos that defines our humanity?

What has been happening in our village?

The following massive culture shifts took place in our village over the last number of years:

- Urbanisation: Between 1950 and 2019 the world's urban population has risen almost sixfold from 751 million to 4,2 billion (World Economic Forum 2019 Report)[3]

- Younger population: 26 percent is under the age of fifteen years old out of a world population of 7,6 billion inhabitants. In Africa it is as high as 41 percent (Statista 2020 Report). [4]
- Poverty and highly uneven distribution of socio-economic opportunities: The inequality gap is unprecedented. The world's 2153 billionaires have more wealth than 4,6 billion people who make up 60 percent of the planet's population (Oxfam International 2020). [5]
- A serious relational crisis characterised by the following:
    - Increasing individualism: The first question that preoccupies people's minds in the village is - What is in it for me? The whole notion of the common good has been completely put on the backburner.
    - Decreasing sociability: We are so extensively connected technologically yet relationally disconnected. We have lost the art of deep and meaningful engagement with each other. Our way of communication takes place primarily through social media where texts, blogs, tweets and the like are the preferred routes to keep in touch. Please do not get me wrong; these are wonderful enablers and I certainly make use of them as well. However, they should never become expedient replacements for meaningful engagement.
    - Increasing materialism: Value judgement is based on externalities such as the car you drive, the clothes you wear, which suburb you live in, your position and status, rather than inner virtues. Charisma has been elevated above character.

The village is crying out for effective leadership. In this context, I want to raise this question very sharply with my fellow villagers – How can we get better leaders whose approach is relevant for our times? I am referring to a type of leadership that is more humane, authentic and capable of affording people a greater sense of meaning. There are just too many of our leaders who are self-serving and do not have hearts of servants. For those of us operating primarily in a part of the village called the developing world, it is of great concern that we will never be able to assert ourselves in the ever-changing world of socio-economic change and rapid technological advancements, with this type of leadership. To leapfrog from the impediments of our current reality into the great possibilities afforded us by the 4th Industrial Revolution, warrants our collective ingenuity and a high degree of effective leadership. The latter is non-negotiable. If not, it will be a missed opportunity that can only result in the persistence of the current global socio-economic disparities with devastating consequences. This will once more entrench the phenomenon of insiders and outsiders.

We are indeed living in turbulent times and unprecedented levels of uncertainty. Peter Drucker made the following statement in this regard, *"A time of turbulence is a dangerous time, but its greatest danger is a temptation to deny reality."* [6] Regrettably, for too long have we succumbed to this phenomenon in South Africa. We are in denial about the trustworthiness and credibility of the ruling elite, the ineptitude and wastage in the public service (R54,6 billion in irregular expenditure according to the latest Auditor General report of 2020), collapse of the public health care system, a high percentage of dysfunctional municipalities, a racially skewed economy where most of the population is still excluded consciously and deliberately and racism in all shapes and forms to name but a few.

One of the greatest responsibilities of leadership is to assist people to move towards a shared perspective of reality. As a leader, you need to realize that there are just so many people who depend on you when you are in a leadership position and your actions can have irreversible consequences. People's fortunes can be wiped out, their hopes shattered, and their development stunted, resulting in a society falling into dysfunctionality and destined for perpetual poverty and deprivation.

A game called power

We are all fascinated by the potential to possess power. Having the power to determine the destiny of a nation, a city, a big corporation, a social movement, or the family legacy can be a very exhilarating experience.

According to David Mc Kenna *"Power is a neutral agent that can be used for good or evil, depending on the mission and motivation of the user."* [7]

If we are to be totally honest, within all of us lurks the desire to be in control. Control is necessary when in a leadership position but here I am specifically referring to negative control informed by selfish ambition. We embark on all manner of diverse tactics to ensure that we are in charge of the situation. On my leadership journey, I made the following observations about the tactics employed by certain leaders to sustain negative control:

1. Personalisation of leadership

When there is a dubious agenda, in the words of Bishop Henry Okullu from Kenya *"Leadership is personalised, and this personalisation leads to idolization of the leader to such an extent that people are made to believe that their rights come from the generosity of their leader."* [8] The dispensing of patronage to a selected network, ensures that they do the leader's bidding regardless of how wrong he or she might be.

2. Power at all costs

When a leader has such an insatiable desire for power, rationality goes out the window. There is an unsubstantiated sense of optimism that does not tally with reality, being risky at best and reckless at worst. Many leaders have taken their followers to fight a war at great cost, informed by nothing else than misplaced obsession with power.

3. Pawns on a chessboard

This emanates from a set of circumstances whereby the leader is controlling or playing with the minds of followers by artful and unfair means to his or her own advantage. This environment of manipulation creates a situation where you always feel threatened. There are also high levels of fear and mistrust. Your default position is to succumb and comply in order not to be on the wrong side of the leader.

We have seen a lot of these examples in our village. It is about time that we give those leaders who are merely playing a game of power a red card and disqualify them. We are dealing with the future sustainability of our village and this power play cannot be allowed to continue indefinitely. For too long have we allowed some leaders to use us as a means towards their own selfish ends. The game needs to be brought to an abrupt end!

Redefining the rules of the game

Being in leadership puts you in an incredibly unique position because your influence can make a major difference in the lives of those that you have been entrusted to lead. It can also assist to set a benchmark worth emulating beyond your current generation. Leadership is not a power game to be played, driven by a mentality of conquest. We are desperately in need of leaders who are real, honest and sincere. It starts from a position of deep introspection. One needs to truthfully respond to this critical question – "Why am I availing myself for a leadership position?" If you do not have a firm grasp of your primary purpose in leadership, all your endeavours will be a glorified ego trip.

One of the greatest leaders that ever walked the face of the earth was Jesus Christ. He completely redefined the rules of the game in leadership. His message to us in Mathew 20: 25 – 26 (The Message MSG) sums up the key differentiator of Jesus' approach to leadership when He conveyed this profound truth to His disciples "*You have observed how godless rulers throw their weight around, how quickly a little power goes to their heads. It's not going to be that way with you. Whoever wishes to be great among you, must become your servant.*"

There is nothing wrong in aspiring for greatness. As a matter of fact, God deposited within you the requisite gifts, talents and abilities to excel in life and set new benchmarks of excellence. The question is – "What is the motivation of your heart?" Is it about constantly being seen, heard and acknowledged? Is it about proving something? Is it about the image you want to project? Is it about misplaced authority and privilege?

Leadership is currently labouring beneath a very shaky reputation. There are however leaders who are an embodiment of greatness because they embraced absolute servanthood. History is also quite instructive in this regard when we reflect on the lives of Mother Teresa, Mahatma Gandhi, Nelson Mandela and Martin Luther King Jr. to name but a few.

You can also become great in your own name and right by being a serving leader as opposed to a self-serving leader.

Some of the greatest people I have encountered in my life are not necessarily high-profile personalities but ordinary men and woman, who through the right motivation of their hearts:

- Give unselfishly of themselves without the expectation of any recognition at all.
- Invest maximum time and effort to unlock potential in others and taking them to places they could never have gone on their own.
- Pursue a cause much bigger than themselves, with a focussed sense of legacy on their minds.

There are many methodologies, theories, self-help material and courses that equip you to master certain techniques to change leadership behaviour. They all serve a useful purpose and I also engaged with several of these on my leadership journey. However, my experience with most of these interventions is that its focus is primarily on external variables whereas leadership is inherently a matter of the heart. Your heart is the centre of your attention, affection, and intention. Our heart gives us the "Why" of embarking on a specific endeavour. If the motivation of our heart is correct, all the other actions will follow suit.

In one of the Lead Like Jesus seminars that I attended a few years ago, Phyllis Hendry confronted us with these piercing questions that really changed my life:

- Who and what do you worship?
- Where is your primary source of security, self-worth and wisdom?
- Who is your primary audience, put differently – what gallery are you playing to? [9]

May I request that you also seriously reflect on these questions. These questions speak to the heart of servant leadership. If after reflection some adjustments need to be made in your life, acknowledge it and ask the Lord to give you the wisdom to deal with it. His grace is sufficient to empower you on your journey towards greatness. We urgently need to set a new standard and model an approach that is directly the opposite of the prevailing one. The village cries out for it. There is a better way.

Lead as He led!

Ecosystem or Ego system?

I had a conversation recently with my good old friend Sam Alexander who gave me a powerful insight on the leadership landscape. He contends that there is an alarmingly shallowness of leadership in South Africa notwithstanding the thousands of graduates emerging from our universities. According to Sam, we are preparing individuals who can excel individually as ego leaders and not individuals who can simulate co – creativity called eco leaders. He made a thought-provoking statement, which I recorded in my notebook: *"Insecurity exists because of what the system rewards."* Insecure people take refuge in silos where they have a false sense of control and create artificial barriers so that their own limitations are not exposed.

In my observation, misguided enforcement of authority and being on an ego trip is a potent cocktail that intoxicates leaders with catastrophic consequences. It leads to a situation where the interaction is primarily transactional in nature and some unwritten contract exists between the leader and followers that is – "You scratch my back and I will scratch yours." Try and disagree with me and you will be simply ignored, victimised, and even asked to leave. The opposite to this kind of approach is to create an environment of community; encouraging the development of relationships where people are valued and can learn from one another; feeding from each other's strengths. In this type of environment, we genuinely embrace diversity and inclusivity. Our endeavours are not just internally focussed but we identify how we can make a meaningful impact on the external environment in which we operate. It is about responding appropriately to an obligation of co-creating a sustainable future. It results in a melting pot of ideas and critical thinking that enriches our collective output.

One of the most difficult challenges for some leaders, is to give power away and not accumulate it. When you want to ensure the future sustainability of an organisation, you must progressively put power where it rightfully belongs, into the hands of the people you lead. The obsessive need for control is rooted in fear, the fear of failure. Followers develop a preoccupation with performance against rigid rules with little margin for innovation. This leads to a grudging sense of compliance instead of a liberating sense of innovation. If they are allowed the space and opportunity of co-creating the solution, they will also take ownership for the results. This enhances their self-esteem and gives them the confidence to take on bigger responsibilities.

Globally and even more pronounced locally, leaders are currently required to navigate extremely turbulent waters. Our political and economic environment is increasingly resembling bungee jumping. Social cohesion is very brittle, technological shifts are mind boggling and the devastating effects of the Covid-19 pandemic are just some of the issues that can become like a horror movie on the screens of many leaders. In my own journey, some of the toughest leadership moments have been when I needed to make a difficult decision and people were looking at me for a plausible solution. In the crucible of these challenging moments, I was always mindful of the wise counsel of Brandon Cox who observed that: *"The best leader in the room is not the one with all the answers."* [10] This stance is by no means an attempt to shy away from one's obligations as a leader but an acknowledgement of the interdependent dynamics on which successful leaders thrive. It is a clear contrast between the ego and eco leadership approach.

Upon reflection, I now realise that in the early stages of my leadership journey, my inclination was more towards the ego kind of approach. As I started to grow, the following guiding principles greatly assisted me to transition more confidently into an eco-leadership environment:

- Follow your inner convictions: What will be the values that will inform my next move?
- Do not fly solo: Over the years I have built up a trusted network of key individuals whose wise counsel I trust and value. Sometimes I need to source in the best possible expertise when the problem is of a specialised nature.

- Counting the costs: What resources need to be deployed, with which alliances do I need to collaborate and what systems need to be activated to successfully deal with the matter?
- Focus: Follow through in a focussed manner on what has been agreed upon. Every team member needs to be on the same page all the time; if not, it will totally disrupt the ecosystem.
- Objectivity: An open and responsive attitude to learning the new and unlearning the old that impedes progress. An admission that I do not know it all and opening myself up for new possibilities.

The value and values of the original village

That powerful African phenomenon Ubuntu has defined us as a people and informed every endeavour in our village over the centuries. It places the emphasis on being through others. It is commonly expressed through the phrase – "I am because of who we all are." Ubuntu is the essence of a human being, the divine spark of goodness inherent within each of us. It inculcates a spirit of interdependence, reciprocity, dignity, the common good and peaceful co-existence. Archbishop Desmond Tutu sums it up so beautifully *"My humanity is bound up in yours for we can only be human together. We are different precisely in order to realize our need of one another."* [11]

Regrettably, there is an increasing spirit of individualism that has become pervasive in our village and the common good has become a secondary consideration. The village has increasingly been taken over by the law of the jungle and survival of the fittest. The collective aspirations that defined us as a people have been adulterated and replaced by Me, Myself, and I. Given some of the vexing socio – economic issues we are confronted with in the global village, warrants a firm moral commitment to the principles of Ubuntu. The time has come for us to move back with urgency to our roots and to what defined us as a people.

Another key feature in African culture is the role of the elders. There has always been a core group of wise elders resident in the village who were trusted, respected, believed and admired in the community. They were the custodians of the history, culture, and values of society. Whenever challenges emerged in the village, they were the first port of call to apply their collective wisdom and give appropriate direction.

One of my best reads during the lockdown period of the Covid-19 pandemic, was a book called Wisdom at Work by Chip Conley. In one of the chapters, he writes about the making of a Modern Elder.[12] These are people who carry with them an air of gravitas blended with a spirit of humility. According to Conley, they possess the following characteristics:

1. Good judgement: This is borne out of experience.
2. Unvarnished insight: They have the ability to cut through the clutter quickly to find the core issue that needs attention.
3. Emotional Intelligence: Wisdom is not only what you speak but the ability to listen with intent and read some of the most important verbal cues. As he puts it so aptly "*Knowledge speaks but wisdom listens.*"
4. Holistic thinking: They grasp the bigger picture much clearer.
5. Stewardship. They know the limitation of their tenure and always approach issues with legacy in mind.

We have neglected these essential principles that defined us as a people and failed to tap into our inherent strengths. We cannot leave it to chance indefinitely. We will be well advised to go back to our roots; take the best out of it and contextualise it for our current set-up.

What are we trying to say to each other? The world has indeed become a global village. There are quite a few cultural shifts that took place in this village that has the potential to adversely affect how we relate to each other. The moral fibre of our village is up for scrutiny. There are also major shifts in the world of work and how business is conducted with a myriad of ground-breaking technological advancements called the 4th Industrial Revolution. It holds great promise but also comes with its own set of serious challenges.

The global village cries out for effective leadership to bring about a more equitable and just society where socio-economic advancement is as inclusive as possible. The question remains – Who raises the village? Who are those amongst us that will influence the thinking, behaviour, and values of the village? We need leaders that we can trust, believe, and respect. Will the Modern Elder within you show up and rise to the challenge?

Chapter 2

A JOURNEY FROM STRUGGLE TO SIGNIFICANCE

Welcome to my village! I will endeavour to colour in the picture of a 65-year journey lived out in my village, as best as I can. It was a hard, challenging, at times contradictory yet life changing journey. Since my days in primary school, I always had destiny on my mind notwithstanding the constraints in my environment. Leadership also came so natural to me.

Admittedly in hindsight, I was not always ready for some of the assignments that were thrust upon me, but I was always up for a challenge. If I can sum it up in a singular thought - it was a journey from struggle to significance. I can wholeheartedly identify with the sentiments expressed by the great King David in Psalm 139: 16 (MSG) *"Like an open book, You watched me grow from conception to birth. All the stages of my life were spread out before You. The days of my life were spread before I'd even lived one day."*

I am the eldest son of the late William and Edna Kuscus and was raised with my seven other siblings in a township called Alabama - Klerksdorp. We were brought up under very impoverished conditions and my dad eked out a living on one of the local gold mines and later got involved as a long-distance truck driver. He was a very industrious man and instilled in me the virtue of hard work. He also played a leading role in matters of church leadership. My mom was more of the disciplinarian but had a big heart and she had the unique ability to always create a very homely environment. We lived in a two bedroomed house with no bathroom and an outside bucket-system toilet but we were quite a happy and content family. I have some great memories of my childhood with my siblings and the environment was quite supportive for us to live as a cohesive family. My parents were always very proud of me because I distinguished myself academically since primary school days and was always number one or at the very least, second in class.

There was however a significant family event when I was in high school. My dad walked out of the house and left us totally destitute. This was a big blow to us and put tremendous strain on the family. Mom had to raise us single- handed and worked extremely hard to provide for us. She had to do washing and ironing or any other menial task in other people's homes just to put bread on the table. I also hustled around for casual jobs on weekends and during school holidays; every bit counted. Mom ultimately got a part time job at a local newspaper – The Klerksdorp Record, where she folded inserts for the papers till the early hours of the morning to pay for my boarding fees and related expenses to get me through matric at Promosa High School in Potchefstroom. Given the tough family conditions, I developed an extremely low self-esteem and veered off into deviant and risky behaviour. In my matric year, I was expelled just about a month before writing my final exams. One of my teachers saw me smoking marijuana in full public view with some very unsavoury characters at a major soccer tournament. He reported it the next Monday to the school principal who summarily dismissed me. My mom had to rush to school a few days later to plead my case with tears in her eyes and I was allowed to continue under extremely strict terms. That year, only three of us passed matric out of a class of 12 and I was one of the three.

I went to the University of Western Cape (UWC) in 1974 to study for a Bachelor of Arts (BA) degree to qualify as a teacher. Dad by that time briefly resurfaced. The year at varsity was very controversial. I started very well with my academic endeavours but in the middle of the first semester,

I secured a part-time job at a liquor supermarket where I earned R12 for Friday afternoons and Saturday mornings. That was serious money for a student by then. A friend of mine and I however saw a gap in the logistics of the store which created an opportunity for us to sell liquor of serious quantities illegally on the side. I became the official "shebeen" at UWC. It was a roller coaster ride at varsity where I was enjoying a bit of a celebrity status albeit for the wrong reasons. When the year ended, I just scraped through academically. I was heading home with a large contingent of students on the Trans Karoo express train on that fateful day of 24 November 1974. The whole coach resembled a varsity rag scene as we were really drinking up a storm throughout the day until late in the evening. Then disaster struck.

I woke up in the morning next to the railway track dazed, bewildered with an excruciating headache and my whole body riddled with pain. I tried to get up but could not because my right leg was broken. After lying there in the hot Karoo sun for an extended period in the middle of nowhere and not being able to get up, a train ultimately passed by, and I raised my hands and screamed to get the driver's attention. A while after that, some people from the railway authorities came to my rescue, arranged for an ambulance and I was hospitalised in a place called Richmond. I suffered a hairline crack on my skull, my right ankle was broken, serious lacerations all over my body and my back resembled a fisherman's net. I was hospitalised there for a week and arrived home in crutches. During the preceding days before my arrival home, there were already rumours circulating in my hometown that I had a fatal train accident. I spent 18 weeks on crutches and was not medically fit to go back in time for the opening at varsity.

At a later court inquest, it was established that I might have walked in my sleep highly intoxicated to the toilet. The toilet was not far from the exit and I mistakenly opened the exit door and walked out of the train that was travelling at high speed by then. Unbeknown to me as I hit the ground, I immediately lapsed into a coma from about midnight until I woke up in the morning. It is unbelievable how I am still alive today. Just thinking about it makes me shudders. Death, paralyzed in a wheelchair, loss of limbs or brain damage could easily have been the outcome. I came to the conclusion that God preserved me because He had a great plan and purpose for my life. By then I did not fully appreciate it because when I recovered, I went back to my old lifestyle again. I used to dance with my crutches to the tune of Marvin Gay's – "Let's get it on." without a care in the world. Notwithstanding my persistent disobedience and recklessness, God did not give up on me. During my recovery period my dad disappeared again without a trace only to make a brief appearance after 25 years at mom's funeral in 1999. I decided to work when I recovered to help mom with the burden of raising the family and spent a few years in industry in Johannesburg.

The nurse from Alabama

At the end of 1976 I returned home from Johannesburg unemployed and without a sense of purpose. Whilst having been hospitalised for a few days at Klerksdorp Hospital, something caught my attention. I saw the male nurses so dignified in their white uniforms and so competent in the things they did that I began to consider this as a profession. When I was discharged, I went straight to the Nursing Service Manager's office to enquire about the prospects of joining the nursing profession. I was met by Mrs Rakumakoe who told me about nursing. What struck me was her cool and calm demeanour as she emphasised: *"My son if you are looking for a job, you have knocked on the wrong door because nursing is a calling."* After listening to her very inspiring life lesson, I was sold out on the idea of joining the profession. Within three weeks after filling in the application forms, I got appointed on 1 March 1977. Initially people thought that I was just playing around because being a male in the nursing profession and being the first one ever from my community, was quite rare during that time.

I spend 17 years in the nursing profession and can without any fear of contradiction say that it has arguably been the most important years of my professional development, that prepared me for my future leadership assignments. I moved through the ranks from being a student nurse to qualify as a professional nurse in 1980. A few years after registration, I studied further and obtained a BA(Cur) degree in nursing education through the University of South Africa and became a lecturer at the nursing college for seven years after which I was promoted into a management position at Tshepong Hospital.

Life is defined by moments. I would like to highlight just two defining moments that took place during this time whilst in the nursing profession. The first one happened in 1979 whilst I was doing night duty shifts for seven successive nights. There was a lady who was then my senior who worked with me. We really worked well together and there was a real chemistry developing between us as we went about our work in this terribly busy surgical ward. When our shifts ended after seven nights, I discovered that I was really missing something badly. You know that mysterious and sometimes confusing part of us that enables us to have moments of quiet laughter, hope and dreams of our lives? You know that heart thing? After the second night of our new shift cycle, I plucked up the courage to try and explain to her what was happening to me. Suffice to say that my proposal was flatly rejected because I had a bit of a notorious reputation. I did not give up and after a few strategically timed approaches, she consented to give it a chance. Guess what, it was such a beautiful journey notwithstanding all the obstacles and challenges; I ultimately tied the knot with Liz on 4 December 1981.

By God's grace we are still going strong and madly in love today. Out of our union, we were blessed with three beautiful children the eldest being Esther, then Ezra and our last born (laat lammetjie) Zoe. I thank the Lord for blessing me with very gifted children. Esther is a strong leader with exceptional organisational skills. Ezra is very entrepreneurial and streetwise whilst Zoe is the creative mind amongst them. Esther married an incredibly good man, Steven Harrison; they are based in Melbourne – Australia and have blessed us with two bubbly grandchildren Naomi and Gabriel. There is nothing that excites me more in life than to hear my grandchildren calling me Oupa! (Grandpa)

The second defining moment happened on the 9 October 1982. As alluded to earlier, I never attended church for a period of 14 years. I began to attend church, albeit with a hidden agenda, just for the dedication ceremony of my eldest daughter. After a few weeks of attending, I realised that this church thing was not so bad after all. On the said night of the

9th of October, I listened to a very powerful sermon delivered by Rennie Magardie. That night was one of the most defining moments of my life when I committed my life to Christ. Liz accepted Christ in her life sometime in 1981 but was not that much into it yet. When she saw the change in me after a few weeks, she really caught the fire again and we were baptised together towards the end of November 1982. From the onset of this journey, I experienced the power of God in such a powerful and unique way. I was totally sold out to the things of God from the onset. I recall that we spent our first winter of marriage in a caravan because of the housing shortage in the township we lived in. The Sunday after being baptised, I sowed my first ever tithe into the Kingdom and the next day we got an opportunity to move into a beautiful flat. I was able to buy Liz a nice stove with an oven and she baked and cooked up a storm for that Christmas. It was also my first Christmas being sober after 15 years.

Tshepong Hospital also heightened my social consciousness. I stayed in a Coloured area as defined by the then apartheid laws. It is no secret that these areas were somehow better resourced than the African townships. Having developed strong friendships with colleagues and frequenting African townships, I got first-hand exposure to their lived realities. It was also a time of great discontent amongst the youth in African townships.

I often worked in the Emergency Department over weekends, which exposed me to the naked brutality of the apartheid army and police forces. People were randomly shot at during the upheavals in the townships as if being hunted down like wild game. The injuries sustained by sometimes elderly people out of these atrocities, never failed to attract my attention and derision. I attended some of the funerals in the African townships which were politically charged with raw passion and emotion. I gradually got sucked into township politics and I want to pay special tribute to some of my political mentors that helped to heighten my passion for social justice. Amongst them is Henry Moleme, the late Sylvia Benjamin, Vusi Moyakhe and Iqbal Motala.

In my own community, I established a civic movement called the Alabama Concerned Residents Association (ACRA). I was elected Chairperson of the structure and our leadership team embarked on a service payment boycott for months, protesting against the bad service delivery in spite of the high rates we paid for it. We became closely aligned with the other progressive structures in the African townships and started high level political conscientisation in my community against a very unjust system. It was an inherently risky yet fulfilling journey because the anger of the people was tangible and almost at boiling point. Thus, we as the leadership needed to steer their anger into something positive. The leadership also featured very prominently on the radar of the notorious Special Branch of the security police and every move had to be well calculated. I also started serving in other alliance structures as Chairperson of the Progressive Primary Health Care Network for Western Transvaal and later the National Health Commission of the African National Congress (ANC). Our home by then resembled a doctor's consulting room as people would be queuing up in the afternoon for assistance on a whole range of issues. The leadership of ACRA became the alternative voice against the apartheid appendages in my community. I attracted the attention of friend and foe alike but there was an increasing sense of expectancy especially after the unbanning of the ANC and the release of Nelson Mandela in 1990.

On a positive note, my family life began to flourish. Both Liz and I made tremendous strides in our professional lives. There was also another exciting development during this time that I will always be thankful about. We were blessed with our own property in 1988. Will I ever forget 27 Benting Street in Alabama, Klerksdorp? My mom managed to get a job at Pick and Pay and her boss, Percy Toorn approached us to take over the rental contract for the house which he was renting for six months with an option to buy it from the owner because he was moving into his own place. Pick and Pay was willing to subsidise half of the rental amount because their contract with the owner still had to run for six months. We were given only 24 hours to decide. We said a simple prayer that night and when we woke up the next morning, we just had this absolute peace in our hearts that it was the right thing to do. We moved in and made an offer to the owner for R57000 which he accepted and we became neighbours to some of the wealthiest people in Alabama. Our application for a bond was approved and we paid the transfer costs.

We were still novices in the property market and did not realise that we still had to pay the bond registration costs of R1460 and not only the transfer costs. In 1988 that was serious money for a civil servant. We tried everything but could not raise the money and the prospect of the transaction being cancelled loomed large in our minds. That afternoon of the deadline, Liz and I went on our knees to pray. As I was having a cup of tea after praying, the name of Dr Chris van Veijeren, a brother from the Hospital Christian Fellowship (HCF), hit me out of the blue. I called him and he invited me to his flat. After I explained to him my predicament, he walked into his bedroom and a few minutes later, handed me a cheque of R2000. I asked him about the repayment, and he said I could start repaying him after a year because he knew that there are still a few things for us to do on the house. The next morning when the lawyers opened, I was there to pay and after a few days I even got my change. With the change, we could replace those ugly deep pink curtains which Esther so disliked. That is how we acquired our first property. God is great!

After all the massive protest actions and the relentless battles we tactically fought with the local authority in Klerksdorp, the local business chambers brought the warring parties together. The municipality of Klerksdorp had the foresight to set up a negotiating mechanism towards the latter part of 1993 to facilitate an orderly transition to a more inclusive local authority. I was selected by the ANC Alliance structures together with two young lawyers Iqbal Motala and Selwyn Silent as chief negotiators. Given the levels of mistrust, it was quite a challenging assignment, but we held our own in the bullring of fierce contestation for political power. It was during this time that I caught the attention of the ANC Provincial leadership based on the gutsy performance our team displayed in the process. I got a call at the beginning of 1994 from Zakes Tolo who was by then the Deputy Chairperson of the ANC in the Western Transvaal, to come and see him at his office. He was heading the elections team and indicated to me that the leadership had decided that I should avail myself as a candidate for the first democratic elections. I requested a few days to give him a response.

I first brokered the idea with Liz, but she had reservations about it since becoming a career politician did not feature on our family's radar. By then I saw my role more of a social activist. The next stop was my spiritual leader Pastor Tim Salmon and after a brief chat, he sent me back to Liz whilst he undertook to reflect and pray about it. His assertion was that you could have the best crowd backing you but if you did not have home base support, it was bound to fail. I set aside time with Liz to address all the concerns and anxieties and I really treasure those moments because it was so engaging and with such a high degree of connectedness and honesty, as we explored our future. Once the decks were cleared at home, I went back to see Pastor Tim. When I gave him a report about my engagement with Liz, he told me that he sensed in his heart that God had destined me for something extraordinary.

He used to call me by the same name my late mom addressed me and said "Johnny boy listen now very carefully to Uncle Tim." He gave me such a fatherly talk which I will never forget and will continue to carry with me for the rest of my life.

Pastor Tim said that since I was about to enter the risky environment of public office, there were 4 P's that I need to guard against:

1. Power: This was my first time being endowed with so much power and if kept unchecked, power had the nasty tendency to corrupt and go to one's head. It then makes you prone to corrupt practices and power if not handled correctly, could destroy you.
2. Popularity: I should never draw my affirmation from the crowds. I should always remember that I am not bigger than the cause and the organisation that I was about to represent had been in existence long before I was even born.
3. Pennies: People with corrupt intent would feed on your weaknesses and the things for which you have a healthy appetite. They would start with small gestures (pennies) and later the favours become bigger (pounds). At some stage you will feel obligated to return the favour until you are ensnared in their trap.
4. Petticoats: Be vigilant how you relate to women and do not use your position of power and influence to take advantage of women; getting entangled in a compromising position. Some of them might even have been deliberately deployed by your rivals and

> they will totally silence your voice by holding that moment of impropriety against you.

These words of wisdom I carried with me for the rest of my life and endeavoured to the best of my ability to live by it.

A place called Mmabatho

We fought a very tough election because it was the first democratic one in the country. The ANC obtained a resounding electoral victory, and I was elected into the first legislature of the North West Province based in Mmabatho (now known as Mahikeng). I was sworn in on the Saturday and within a space of four days, my life was turned upside down. The following Wednesday, Premier Popo Molefe called us all into a room and after a lengthy speech, explained to us the challenges and complexities of building a province from scratch and the legitimate expectations of our people for a better life after years of neglect. He then announced his first Cabinet. Most of the names read out were predictable because these were all men and women with impressive credentials in the struggle-movement. But when he came to number seven, I could not believe my ears. He announced that the Finance portfolio goes to Martin Kuscus!! I hardly heard the names of the last three as my mind went into a spin. I did not even know a debit from a credit. Here was I, a nurse a few days ago being called upon to manage R5,2 billion. I phoned my wife later the evening to tell her that we would be moving to Mmabatho.

It is quite difficult to describe to you how I felt immediately after my appointment and the first few days in office. It was a mixed bag of excitement on the one hand but also anxiety, as I contemplated the awesome responsibility that was thrust upon me. It was the biggest move in my lifetime. You have got to live it to describe it. I had to get used to the idea of being chauffeur driven with bodyguards in attendance. I moved into quite a big ministerial residence guarded permanently by a policeman. All the attention of the media and protocols at official functions, was a massive adaptation for my family and me.

I had to constantly remind myself that all these appendages were not what I was elected to do in Mmabatho. I came there to make a small contribution towards changing the lives of those on whose behalf I derived my mandate to serve. It was also not an orderly handover of authority by the previous regime. We had to find our way very quickly. In my case, being deployed to head up the Provincial Treasury and taking multi-million Rand decisions for the first time in my life, was a daunting experience. Talk about faith? Mine was really tested to the limits.

The Lord really gave me wisdom to recruit a core group of competent executive managers, put the necessary policies and procedures in place and revamp the systems to deliver on the vision of the new administration. We really succeeded in building a well-run Treasury which became one of the top performing departments in the province. What was quite surprising to note was when we met for our first gathering of provincial Members of the Executive Council (MEC's) of Finance, only one of my counterparts Prof Mayathula – from Eastern Cape, understood the language of finance and economics. None of us had any previous experience of financial management and economics. The best thing that could happen to us was the appointment of Trevor Manuel as Minister of Finance in 1996; only to discover that he himself also did not have any financial management background. He turned out to be arguably one of the best Cabinet ministers ever in our country's history and a leading figure in world economic affairs. He invested quite a lot in us and developed us into what he proudly referred to as Team Finance.

I was privileged to be part of the team that built a very sophisticated and robust intergovernmental fiscal relations system in the first phase of our democracy. Minister Trevor Manuel was also appointed at a time when the economy threatened to spiral into a debt trap. It was really a proud moment when I had the privilege to attend Parliament as he delivered the Budget Speech in 2007 in which he announced for the first time in the history of our country, a budget surplus - a feat never to be repeated. It is rather sad to see that all our sacrifices and hard work has been squandered and the country is now drowning in unprecedented levels of debt again. He really instilled in me the desire for excellence and being diligent in managing the public purse. I will forever be indebted to the support and mentorship I received from Premier Molefe and Minister Manuel. They both have a strong pedigree from the mass democratic movement and that constantly reminded me of the sacrifices many people made for us to gain political freedom. I dared not fail the trust and confidence placed in me by these luminaries.

It was also during my time in Mmabatho that I lost one of my anchors in life. My mom was on retirement for about two years and staying all by herself. We planned to have her move in with us when Esther finished her matric exams that year. She was a known diabetic for many years and one Saturday night towards the end of October 1999 she was admitted to Tshepong Hospital when she almost lapsed into a hypoglycaemic coma. We went to see her on the Sunday morning and she was in high spirits. We spent quite a bit of time with her that morning and she virtually had a word for each one of us. Firstly, expressing her utmost appreciation for the way Liz and I were taking care of her and making a passionate plea to me to look after Liz. She then turned to Esther and wished her well for the upcoming exams the next Friday. She even joked that she should not die then because she did not want to be blamed if Esther were to fail her matric exams. She then spoke to Ezra and told him, that as our only son, he had the responsibility to carry the family name with honour after me. Little Zoe who was still in primary school, made her a beautiful card of well wishes and she spoke blessings over her. We had a lot of laughter and soaked up every word she spoke to us.

Unfortunately, that was the last time we saw mom. I had planned to visit her in hospital on the Tuesday on my return from a the quarterly MEC's meeting with the Minister of Finance in Pretoria. Whilst on the road to the meeting at about 0600 that morning of the 2 November 1999, the hospital phoned and informed me that mom had passed away at 0430 after a sudden cardiac arrest. She was still chatting the previous night on the phone to us and by all indications the glucose levels were stabilising. We gave her a very dignified funeral which was one of the biggest funerals held in Alabama for a long time. That week I came to realise the impact that my mom commonly known as Ouma Edna had on the community of Alabama. The outpouring of love from the people of Alabama for my mother during our time of bereavement was quite encouraging and made me feel proud to have been brought up in that community.

The following personality traits of my mom, will always stay with me and I will cherish it deeply:

1. Her stubborn faith and dedicated prayer life. When I drifted away from the Lord, she never stopped praying for me for almost 14 years. She and Liz were very close since our courting days. They used to go together to prayer meetings on Wednesday nights whilst Liz was still a student nurse, and it was during one of those meetings that Liz accepted the Lord Jesus into her life. It used to annoy me when the two of them would get up at 0500 in the morning and started praying aloud in mom's bedroom. Without fail, my name always featured in their prayers and that shaped my wife's burden for prayer till today.
2. Notwithstanding her own financial constraints, her generosity of spirit knew no bounds.
3. She always saw the good in others and was a great encourager.

I am glad that she could see the results of her sacrifices in my life during her lifetime. She was present listening with tears in her eyes to me preaching my first sermon at a Wednesday night prayer meeting in 1984. She saw how God prospered me in my professional career and how our family was thriving through God's favour. One of her greatest moments of joy was when I was elected as the first MEC of Finance in the North West Province. We had the privilege of spending her last Christmas together at our place in Mmabatho.

In the party-political arena, I also made great strides and served firstly in the Provincial Executive Committee (PEC) and was later elected Provincial Treasurer between 2000 - 2003. I also succeeded in implementing a strong anti - corruption strategy in the North West which resulted in rooting out corrupt officials. I still have a very vivid picture of one of the headlines in the local newspaper The Mafikeng Mail - Martin "the hitman" Kuscus strikes again. This did not go down well with certain people with corrupt tendencies in the party. I went to the ANC Provincial

Conference in June 2003 with an impressive track record of having turned the financial health of the party around and being one of the star performers in government. Unbeknown to me, there was a speed trap waiting for me at that conference. I lost the Treasurer position by 11 votes in a shocking election result. Before the conference, there were already murmurs on the ground about how certain groupings planned to deal with me at the conference because through the anti - corruption initiatives I had implemented, a few high-profile political figures were exposed and dismissed. I was too naive to think that politics is only about performance per the party mandate. It was a devastating and very humiliating blow for me because when I presented my Treasurer's Report at the conference, I received a standing ovation. However, in a matter of two hours the tide turned against me at the conference. I remember how I was literally crying as I drove home after the conference results were announced. I began asking God serious questions - How could He allow me to be humiliated in this fashion after having worked so hard?

I don't know if it also happens in your life; you pray and it feels that your prayers just hit the ceilings? This happened to me after that conference. Only after two weeks when in prayer and meditating on the Word that the Holy Spirit started ministering to me in such an instructive manner. The Lord reminded me about the days when I entered politics and depended upon Him for every move that I made. As I moved up into the echelons of power, some of the very things Pastor Tim warned me about, started to subtly infiltrate my life. I became so powerful by virtue of my portfolio and being part of the top officials in the party that I became a professional politician; know-it-all, fierce in debates, forceful in driving processes and not suffering fools at all. My prayer life became shallow, family responsibilities sometimes took a backseat and whilst I thought I was making waves, there had developed an increasing gap between me and those I purportedly led because I was obsessed with success. The Lord was no more consulted in most of my endeavours and prayers became a matter of habit. The question raised very sharply by the Holy Spirit to me was – "How can God be blamed for what happened to me in Rustenburg when for a few years now, He was taken out of the driver's seat and occupied the back seat of the car like a tourist?" I could not help myself from the tears flowing during this encounter, this time not of having been allegedly let down by God but tears of remorse and repentance. I was reminded that He is a jealous God; He will not allow His glory to be contended for by anybody or anything. I moved on in my political career with greater success and fruitfulness after the reset button was strategically pressed in Rustenburg.

The 2004 elections were at hand, and I had to decide whether I wanted to continue as MEC of Finance or not. The department was running well, and my portfolio increasingly started to become a maintenance job. When your name appears on the wall of Leopard Park Golf Club as an honorary member, then you know your time is up.

Liz also made huge strides in her professional life by being appointed as Nursing Service Manager at a private hospital in Mmabatho. She also graduated with a degree in Nursing Administration, so we were well settled. The children were thriving as we navigated through the challenging teenager years with the two older ones. As this decision was becoming an elephant in the room, we decided to go out for a week to a place in Modimolla for a retreat concerning direction about the next phase of our lives. After intense engagements, prayer and meditation, there was a strong confirmation in our hearts that our season in Mmabatho was about to end and God was leading us into a new season. At that stage we did not know the details at all except that it was time to move on.

When we returned, I approached my Premier to notify him of my intention not to seek another term in political office. He referred me to the Secretary General (SG) of the ANC who then was Comrade Kgalema Motlante. I came to the party Headquarters -Luthuli House and presented my request for an exit to the SG. Though a bit disappointed initially, his response was quite profound. I will never forget his closing remarks after our session *"Comrade Martin, you really served the organisation with honour."*

I can indeed say that my tenure as MEC of Finance was a serious learning opportunity, a crucible of character development and a time of abundant grace. I still hold the distinction with my counterpart from Gauteng Province Jabu Moleketi, as the longest serving MEC's of Finance in the country. Heads were rolling all over the place but through God's grace I finished two successive terms strongly with no scandals or skeletons in the cupboard.

CHAPTER 2

Poisoned chalice or champaigne glass?

When leaders in the corporate world learned that I was in the market for a job, I was inundated with some very lucrative offers especially from the financial services sector. This was the early wave of affirmative action and experienced Black executive talent was in short supply. We were at the Million Dollar Golf Tournament at Sun City, when a very senior person in government approached me about an exciting position. I gave him my contact details and a few weeks after that, I was approached by the appointed recruitment agency. I went through the very stringent interview processes at the beginning of the year and was successful. But there was a long waiting period because this was a Cabinet appointment and government was in transition to the 3rd administration. I was getting nervous because I only had thirty days left to vacate my official residence in Mmabatho. I ultimately got a call from the Director General of Trade and Industry on a Wednesday afternoon that I had been appointed by Cabinet as the new Chief Executive Officer (CEO) of the South African Bureau of Standards (SABS) for a 5 -year term on 14 June 2004. I met the Chairperson of the Board the next day and because they did not have a CEO for approximately 7 months, he requested me to start the next Monday. We were at that time busy building a house in Hartbeespoort and the contractors were put under great pressure to complete the remaining work within a month.

I accepted the position at SABS because I am not a maintenance-type person and the position posed an interesting challenge. One of my strengths is to build organisations from the ground-up or fix those that are in distress to function at optimal levels. I was able to build a well-functioning Treasury from scratch in my last assignment and armed with that type of experience, I thought that I will be in good shape for the SABS job. I was not aware that I had walked into a war zone. Just three weeks before my arrival, there was a nasty shooting incident on site. One of the staff members lost his disciplinary appeal hearing and nobody knew that he had a gun with him during the Human Resources clearance process. He went to collect his personal belongings and pretending to go and greet colleagues, he walked into his manager's office, fired two shots at her and turned the gun on himself. He died on the scene and the manager died the next day in hospital. My predecessor also left under very controversial circumstances. When I walked in, the air was loaded with fear and suspicion; you could almost cut it with a knife. The prevailing set of circumstances in the organisation was symptomatic of a transformation effort that went terribly wrong.

The SABS was one of the prestige institutions in South Africa having been populated with very resourceful people in the scientific and engineering fields, some of them world leaders in own name and right. Prior to my arrival, the institution was forever in the media for the wrong reasons. There was serious neglect of its client base and public confidence in the institution was at an all - time low. I spent the first few weeks just listening and visiting the then sites where over 1600 staff members were deployed, talking to industry bodies and some of our major clients, other government agencies and regulators. There were quite a lot of contradictions in these interactions as to what led to the demise of SABS and what might be some of the immediate remedial actions.

I embarked on a process of stabilising the internal environment. My approach was informed by this realisation – SABS cannot face its tomorrow unless it dealt with its yesterday because the hurt and divisions were running deep. I want to pay special tribute to Dr David Molapo, Dr Khetso Mabusela and Oom Blackie Swart that facilitated a successful process on what an ideal SABS should look like. In this process, we held small focus group discussions where we challenged all paradigms that were dragging SABS down and inhibit the organisation to function at its optimal potential. There was a 91% participation rate in this process but not without its own challenges. There were tears, hugs and confessions of harbouring wrong views about each other. Others just simply walked out of the meetings because they could not face the reality under the guise of the process being vindictive. To many participants it was a painful yet healing process. It was as if we took the lancet to open the festering boil and cleaning it up for us to be future fit. Some of the lessons learned in this process include:

- Not all the solutions reside necessary at the top. By opening space and opportunity in these focus group discussions, many excellent inputs came from operational staff that were implementable with minimum effort. These quick wins helped with maintaining momentum of the process. We were also able to identify champions amongst the ordinary rank and file to drive the change processes at ground level.
- Do not underestimate corporate culture. I had to respect the values different from my own, through honest engagement. People will accept change if their views are respected. Regard each assignment as an opportunity for mutual learning.
- There must be consistency at the top. Within 5 months of being appointed, one of the executives defrauded the company credit card and he was shown the door. The same action was taken with the Human Resources executive when she got entangled in impropriety.
- Change is a process, not an event. You must however be fanatical to follow through on agreed objectives and targets.
- Everybody must be on the same page through frequent and honest feedback. It will disarm rumour mongers but empower people to own the process. I had fortnightly sessions called "A Moment with Martin" with randomly selected groups from the total staff spectrum. Our engagement was based on how they experienced the change management process by framing it around only 3 Questions: What happened? What's missing? What's next? This greatly assisted with unblocking processes that impeded progress and served as a valuable platform for peer learning.
- Make a big song and dance about every measurable milestone reached, it helps to foster team spirit.

At the end of the process, we agreed on a five- year roadmap with an endorsement from all the staff. During my tenure, we were able to bring the institution back to being one of the top ten certification bodies in the world, increased profitability, increased output on standards development, strong transformation drive, major business process reengineering, expanded our footprint into 18 countries and a major improvement on customer experience. My last assignment was to open a satellite office in Shanghai to do pre-export verification assessments of specifically electrotechnical, cement and automotive products. In 2006 I was elected to serve for a two -year term on the International Standards Council (ISO) based in Geneva, the highest industrial standards authority in the world.

SABS accorded me a major learning opportunity. In my previous position as MEC of Finance in the North West, we received about 80% of the revenue from National Treasury as intergovernmental fiscal transfers and only raised 20% of our own revenue. Whereas at the SABS 88% of its revenue was raised from commercial activities and only 12% from government grants. It instilled in me a new sense of being entrepreneurial through driving down costs, developing new markets and increasing profitability. I also had to contend with increased competition in the certification and testing arenas. It was indeed a great training ground to test my entrepreneurial capability.

My tenure at SABS was quite a busy one. I was appointed by President Mbeki in 2004 to the Finance and Fiscal Commission as a part time commissioner for 5 years. There was however a call that triggered a major move in my life. Whilst being at a standards conference in Nagoya – Japan, I got a call sometime in July 2006 from Trevor Manuel indicating that they were about to appoint the first Board of Trustees and the Presidency had cleared my name to be the first Chairperson of the Board of Trustees for the Government Employees Pension Fund (GEPF) for a three - year term. On my return, I signed the acceptance letter, got elected and it was only after the first meeting that I appreciated the awesome responsibility that I had been assigned to. I was charged with exercising stewardship over a portfolio of R920 Billion!! It was by then the seventh biggest pension fund in the world. My last budget in the North West was only R23 billion.

There were some valuable learning experiences during my tenure at the GEPF. I would just like to highlight a few:

- We established the Pan African Infrastructure Development Fund (PAIDF) with other private sector players and development finance institutions. The primary objective was to finance infrastructure development that would enhance economic development on the African continent. It was a $ 625 million fund, and I was elected as the First Chairperson from 2007 – 2009.

- The GEPF was a founding signatory of the United Nations Principles on Responsible Investment (PRI). I was invited by the then Secretary General of the United Nations the late Kofi Anan, to the signing ceremony at the New York Stock Exchange held on 27 April 2007. The world's top 36 pension funds were in attendance. After three weeks, I got a call from the Director of UNEP a division of the United Nations Global Compact – Paul Clemens Hunt, requesting me to serve on the UN Board for PRI. I served for a three-year term and this gave me arguably some of my best learning experiences on international best practices regarding corporate governance and optimisation of the investment value chain with special emphasis on environmental sustainability, social equity and good governance (ESG).
- Under my leadership, we crafted the Developmental Investment Strategy for impact investments for the GEPF as early as 2009.
- On the 9 June 2008 I had the privilege of participating as a panellist in a thematic debate at the United Nations on Global Capital and Climate Change. I spoke on behalf of all the pension funds in the world with a special emphasis on the impact of climate change on developing countries. It took me 18 hours to fly to New York but only spoke for 12 minutes (my friend you can go and check on Google, I was there!) After that debate, we went for a working lunch and guess who rocked up to address us? The former Secretary General of the United Nations, Ban Ki - moon. He later came to greet all the panellists and as we shook hands, we both noticed that we were wearing identical powder blue Dunhill ties. Do not ever accuse me of not having a proper dress sense.

As I walked out of the UN Building onto the busy streets of New York that day, I could not help thanking God for His favour on my life. I told the Lord that I could not manage anymore surprises. After all, what had I done to deserve it? At that moment, my mind was captivated by a statement that was made by Jentezen Franklin just two months before, when he addressed our annual church conference at Rhema – Randburg. He said *"God only blesses where His reputation is safe."* It was as if the Lord wanted to remind me that if He can trust me with His reputation and if I not wilfully and deliberately bring it into disrepute, He would take me to places and positions of authority that I never dreamt of.

The period between 2004 – 2009 was perhaps the busiest time of my life. Juggling between my fulltime job as CEO of SABS with all its local and international travelling pressures, the work at the Government Employee Pension Fund, Pan African Infrastructure Development Fund, Finance and Fiscal Commission, International Standards Organisation, The United Nations PRI Board…I still do not know how I coped but it gave me massive market exposure and invaluable learning experiences, both locally and internationally. I also saw Luke 16: 10 (New Living Translation NLT) being increasingly fulfilled in my life, declaring: *"If you are faithful in little things, you will be faithful in large ones. But if you are dishonest in little things, you won't be honest with greater responsibilities."*

In your rejection, you will find direction

The jet-set life was just becoming too much and when my contract at the SABS expired, I stayed on till September 2009, but decided not to renew it. By then I already devoted 32 years of my life to the public service. The question I had to grapple with was – "Martin quo vadis?" The response to this question was also informed by a challenging set of events. Allow me to explain.

Before my exit from SABS, I was approached by a large company that was listed on the Johannesburg Stock Exchange that had embarked on an international expansion strategy and the CEO was overstretched. The company wanted to appoint a Managing Director to look after the South African operations. Negotiations were at an advanced stage and terms were close to being finalised. Out of the blue, I received a call from the Chairperson of the organisation telling me that he and the CEO had met that afternoon and had reconsidered their offer and decided not to proceed with filling the position. I just thought okay, no problem, you approached me, I did not apply for any position with you.

My term of office was also about to expire at the GEPF in September 2009. The Deputy Chairperson by then was Dave Balt. Together we went to see the then Minister of Finance – Pravin Gordhan, to give him a close out report of the Board's work during our term of office. We spent a considerable amount of time with him and he was very impressed with the amount of work that we had done as the first Board. We also shared with him our views about critical reforms to be undertaken moving forward. The Minister in that meeting categorically requested both of us to stay on the Board to maintain continuity. I acceded to his request, but Dave declined because he had already made plans for his retirement. Surprisingly, a few weeks after our meeting, the Minister announced the new members of the GEPF Board in Parliament, but my name was excluded from the list. Again, I told myself it's okay, no problem, you requested me Mr Minister, I did not ask you for the position.

My Chairpersonship at the PAIDF was linked to my appointment with the GEPF. Since there was a vacancy on their Board when I was about to exit the GEPF, I was approached by a high- level delegation of the PAIDF Board to avail myself to continue on their Board. I had to submit my Curriculum Vitae (Just imagine, I had successfully launched this organisation under my watch which was operational for two years, but I still had to submit a CV?) and the Board would have pronounced on my appointment by mid - November. Till today, no one has had the courtesy to inform me of the outcome.

I successfully secured the host status for the ISO General Assembly to be held in South Africa in October 2009. This was after fierce international competition, but we managed to have Cape Town declared the host city; the first time the ISO General Assembly was held on the African continent. I was graciously invited by the leadership of SABS to be a special guest at this conference. On my arrival at the hotel, I was immediately approached by a former colleague Joe Bhatia from the USA who told me that they had a crisis because the President-elect, had withdrawn his candidacy. Joe had the mandate to approach me to avail myself for the President-elect position given the fact that I was not in the employ of SABS anymore. According to Joe, the key members in ISO was aware that I had built a respectable profile in the standardization arena and had acquitted myself well with the inner workings of ISO during my tenure on the Council. According to him and the other countries, I would be a perfect fit. I told him to first speak to the South African delegation to obtain their support. The very people, some of whom I had appointed in these powerful positions during my tenure, declined the request to support my candidature which was backed by the seven permanent member countries on the ISO Council. Their response really devasted me as well as the sponsors of the whole initiative. The latter's contention was that it was arguably Africa's best or even last chance (in their own words) to field a credible candidate to become President of ISO.

It was just natural for me to start connecting the dots and ask critical questions as these episodes played itself out one after the other. Why this? What had I done? How come the people whom I trusted, some in whom I had invested so much, could do this? This instilled in me such a deep sense of rejection, having been on such a high for the preceding five years. It almost felt like an adrenaline withdrawal. All of us have a need for approval and acceptance. It is very traumatic to be deliberately marginalized, ostracized and just simply being ignored. The marketplace can be a ruthless space, where certain people for reasons best known to them, could conjure up the worst kind of things to make one feels totally rejected.

I must admit that I lapsed into quite a couple of pity parties when all these things were racing through my mind. One morning at the beginning of February 2010 while preparing myself to speak at the Under African Skies Conference at Crystal Church later that week, a word captivated my mind so intensely that was indeed a game changer: In your Rejection, you will find Direction. As I meditated on this word, I burst into tears and started to confess all the negative thoughts I was harbouring against the people who were key players in the events mentioned earlier. I came to realise that I am not defined by their opinions, and I am not beholden to their approval. I started to reflect on all the exhilarating moments of God's favour on my life, things I never even thought or dreamt about. I got so absorbed as I studied The Bible about the many examples of people who found direction in their rejection and changed the direction of history for example Joseph, Moses, Ruth, David, Rahab, to name but a few. What an uplifting time and a beautiful encounter between me and my Creator.

When I was just about to complete my sermon preparation, my phone rang. A lady answered and identified herself as being an official from the Parliamentary Pension Office. She mentioned that Parliament had made a special provision during the previous year for people that had 10 years' service or more in parliamentary service as a pension gratuity and my province was the last one to be processed. She explained to me the background in order for me to give an appropriate response. The information came through after 10 minutes of dropping the call and I was absolutely dumbfounded. I was given a R1,8 million gratuity and I had an option to reinvest it in a preservation fund or cash in. It was a no brainer, I decided to cash in the gratuity. We got a tax directive from the South African Revenue Service and guess what; the net cash equivalent was approximately what I earned in one year's net salary at SABS. Without any financial pressures, I did not have to be desperate and scavenge around for opportunities. Soccer World Cup 2010 here we come!

In June that year, whilst relaxing and watching rugby on a Saturday afternoon, I received a call from Samuel Ogbu – the CEO of Liberty Properties. He offered me the position of Chairperson for a newly established property fund called Synergy Income Fund, in which Liberty had a substantial interest. I joined the Board towards the beginning of July 2010, and we worked flat- out towards being listed. On 14 December that year, I had the privilege to blow the ceremonial kudu horn as we took that company to a listing on the Johannesburg Stock Exchange. This was another milestone that I would never forget.

In October of 2010, I also got headhunted to be the Chairperson of the Mineworkers Provident Fund. After my appointment, I was immediately tasked with a massive responsibility as we moved the fund from one of the country's biggest fund administrators and established our own administration platform with 148000 members. I spent almost 9 years as Chairperson of the fund and under my watch we received eight successive clean audits, grew the fund from R16 billion – R29 billion, won several industry awards for stakeholder relations, investment performance and a major improvement in the member experience.

There were quite a few other directorships that followed but currently I am a director for the last twelve years on the Board of Netcare – the largest private health care group in Africa. I also serve on the Boards of Ellies Holdings, Liberty Corporate Umbrella Funds and Bigen Africa. I also have some of my own business interests in the telecoms, technology, and organisational development space.

History is also very instructive about people who experienced rejection but ultimately made it to the top and became game-changers. They include:

1. Beethoven's teacher declared him hopeless as a composer.
2. Walt Disney was fired by his newspaper editor for his alleged lack of imagination.
3. Michael Jordan was dropped from his high school basketball team.
4. Steve Jobs was fired unceremoniously from the company he founded.
5. Albert Einstein's parents thought he was mentally handicapped because he did not speak until he was four years old.

How to respond when your mind is captivated by a sense of rejection:

- Do not get into an academic thesis about it. Most of the times it might not even have anything to do with you. It might well be that people cannot come to grips with their own internal issues and project it on to you. Do not become too conspiratorial about it. It is not worth it to spend a lot of negative energy trying to understand it and why it happened?
- Depersonalize the episode. You are not defined by your current reality. You are an Olympic champion in training, whose path to the winner's podium is a long and challenging, yet life changing one. Your life experiences and mine, is the foundation on which authentic leadership is shaped.
- Do not become an honorary member of the Alliance of the Wounded. Surround yourself with people whose judgment you trust; leveraging objective feedback helps to put things into perspective.

- Remain focused on the bigger picture. Your temporary setback can greatly assists in you tapping into your inner resources and make tactical adjustments to stay on course.
- Guard your heart and never allow any bitterness to take root in your life. Pastor Ray McCauley likes to say, *"it's like drinking poison and expecting the other person to die."* If you allow it, it will become like a big hole with many tunnels to get lost in it. This will make the return journey even more difficult.
- Maintain an attitude of gratitude. Call to remembrance all the good and positive things that are happening in your life. There is no better antidote for rejection like gratitude.

The greatness of leadership is in its humility. Rejection has this rare ability to develop genuine humility in us. Numbers 12: 3 (New King James Version NKJV) reminds us: "*The man Moses was very humble, more than all men who were on the face of the earth.*" What would you like to be remembered for? Are you bitter, vengeful, cynical, or have an overly critical spirit? Take it from me, in your rejection, you will find direction.

Stories are very powerful, and they also have the ability to activate us into a specific course of action. It also has the power to invite others into your space to become part of something much bigger than themselves. I trust that by giving you a synopsis of my own story, that it will inspire, heal, restore, redirect, and just challenge you afresh that you are made for more. God made each of us incredibly unique and we have a particular story to tell the world about His love, faithfulness, and mercy in our respective lives. Mine is a story of a leader that was at some stage totally lost but once again through God's grace, have been found.

You are not defined by your current reality. Some people might have even given you a name with negative connotations about it. It's okay, they don't know your full story. Whatever trials and challenges you are currently going through now, is part of God's preparation to equip you so that your life experiences will one day inspire, motivate, and challenge others in their journey of life. It certainly happened in my life, and I am sure He can do it for you as well.

Chapter 3

CREDIBILTY – THE DNA OF EFFECTIVE LEADERSHIP

In the previous chapter, I attempted to give a snapshot of my life; from obscurity to the commanding heights of power and influence. I am sure that by now, you may be asking "I wonder how this guy got it right?" I am glad you are asking. Some people might think I was lucky, others might ascribe it to being politically connected or whatever reason one might advance. If truth be told, it is a combination of many things but if I need to sum it up in one singular thought – Credibility was the DNA that kept me going in a world in which compromise reigns supreme. My simple understanding of DNA (deoxyribonucleic acid) is that it is a vitally important molecule not only for humans but for most other organisms as well. It is the carrier of genetic information. Drawn from this analogy, I would respectfully submit that credibility is indispensable for effective leadership.

What do I mean by credibility? The word credibility comes from the Latin word credere, which means – to believe. What this implies is that when you have credibility, people start to believe in you because you consistently follow through on what you have pronounced upon. It is that attitude of heart where you are truthful to who you really are and being genuine and sincere in your commitments and intentions. You engage with the world in a unique and authentic manner, remaining faithful to your inner convictions and not a proxy for external agendas. You are the real deal, nothing pretentious about you and being comfortable in your own skin. From a leadership perspective, credible people are not only believed but they are trusted, admired, and respected. Regrettably, there are just too many people out there parading as leaders, that simply cannot be believed because they are merely acting out a role that is not reflective of who they really are.

Needless to say, the world is yearning for credibility; it yearns for genuine, real and sincere people. By this I am not propagating perfectionism but an attitude of relational integrity. As I moved up the leadership ladder, I encountered just too many poor representations of leadership, and this instilled in me a desire not to go that route. My days of performing in school concerts are over. What you see is what you get.

I once watched a video clip a few years ago, in which the senior game ranger narrated how the white rhino was under a severe threat in the Pilanesberg National Park. He reported that whilst on their morning patrols, they would frequently find a white rhino against the fence or nearby bushes, severely stressed, panting for air and severely injured. What was however baffling, was that the rhino's horn remained intact. This was obviously not an attempt at rhino horn poaching but motivated by something else. They decided to install surveillance equipment at strategic points in the park and to their horror, video footage revealed that there was a gang of young elephants marauding at night, targeting a lone rhino. They would chase it all over the park and then viciously attack it when it ran out of steam.

After careful consideration, management realized that the problem started almost seven years prior to the reported incidents. There was an over – population of elephants in the Kruger National Park; a sizeable amount was culled, and some transferred to Pilanesberg. Instead of bringing the whole herd, they only brought the young ones to save on logistical costs. What should however be noted is that in animal life, territorial dominance is a critical factor. Since the young ones were not under the authority of a dominant bull, they engaged in, for lack of a better word "un-elephant" behaviour. To save the problem, a few bulls were brought into Pilanesberg. Within a matter of two weeks, this deviant behaviour of the young ones was nipped in the bud due to the visible presence of authority.

This narrative sensitized me to one of the major causative factors that are undermining acceptable societal norms and standards - the lack of credible authority. It manifests itself in weird and sometimes behaviour that is unheard-of with quite detrimental consequences in business, politics, family life, church circles. education, sport - you name it.

South Africa is a country of great promise and possibility. Regrettably, our country has increasingly become a world leader in divorce, violent crime, drug - and alcohol abuse. We have witnessed a massive escalation in femicide and child abuse over the last decade. The country is beset by stubborn levels of poverty, inequality, and unemployment after almost three decades of political freedom.

To confront some of the vexing socio – economic challenges as well as an increasing erosion of our moral fibre, warrants credible authority not only on the political front but in all spheres of society. By this I mean the kind of authority that can be believed, trusted, admired and respected. As could be seen in our Pilanesberg example, the presence of credible authority engenders appropriate behaviour and stability.

Presence is vital in leadership

The concept of presence in leadership is difficult to define, almost like the concept of beauty; you know it when you encounter it. The best example I can think of to illustrate the point, was during the 1995 Rugby World Cup Final at the Ellis Park stadium. I had the privilege to be at the venue when Nelson Mandela walked into a packed stadium filled with mostly White South Africans, wearing a number six Springbok rugby jersey. His mere presence generated a highly emotional response of love and affirmation. It irreversibly confirmed his status as the President of a new democratic South Africa for all its people. To crown it all, the Springboks won the World Cup trophy that day. What a historical day in the life of our new nation.

Leaders with presence communicate vision, inspiration, passion, and assertiveness with grace and without any tinge of arrogance. When you are near them, they exude warmth and are approachable. They maintain high levels of emotional intelligence and are not ruffled by peripheral matters. People can be assured that they will enjoy the leader's undivided attention when interacting with him/ her; being present in the moment.

In my leadership journey, I always made a genuine and sincere attempt without being overbearing at all, to ensure that my presence is felt in a real and meaningful way. If you do not maintain that as a leader, the people you lead will feel disconnected and this will erode credibility of your authority. One of my mentors John Stanbury once told me "Martin the last time people spoke the truth to you was when you were appointed as CEO. Henceforth, all information coming to your desk will be filtered." It is your responsibility to do a few dipsticks at times to acquaint yourself about the factual situation at ground level and engage with the people you are leading out of genuine and sincere considerations. What you model at the top, will define the credibility of your leadership. This needs to be at the top of your mind all the time because leadership is not merely taught, it is also caught.

Building the brand in you

Brands are basically an idea or image of a specific product or service that customers connect with. A lot of time and resources are spent to create and maintain a brand. In the year 2020, Amazon was rated as the top global brand and its brand value was estimated to be worth close to $220 billion.

The consumer market is a very dynamic and sophisticated space. I listened to a radio talk show programme recently where it was said that the average consumer is exposed to about 5000 advertising messages per day. Consumers are spoilt for choice and wields enormous power in their buying decisions. They seek a brand that makes them feel appreciated, understood, and worthy to be identified with. If these boxes can be ticked, brand loyalty becomes an enduring one.

The key differentiator in the whole scheme of things, is the issue of credibility. The product should be something of undisputed origin, genuine, real, and veritable. When something is credible, it is not at variance between promise and performance; there is absolute consistency. You cannot fool customers indefinitely. You might initially get away with hyped sales talk and expedient pricing considerations but very soon, they will know intuitively if something is not the real deal. People are constantly in search of reality and will always believe in something that is genuine.

You are a brand! Every day, people create perceptions about you and based on these perceptions (positive or negative) they decide on how to relate to you. You therefore need to take a conscious decision daily, about what you would offer the world. What is so special and unique about you that can be imparted into the lives of those around you? What can I do to genuinely connect with people and not just embark on all manner of endeavours in a desperate effort to impress them? What is your worth and how do you value yourself? In a world with such a myriad of distractions, you will only be taken note of and taken seriously in life, if you maintain credibility.

"Brands are created by impressions that, over time, create a picture of who we are in the minds of our audience, no matter who they are. Everything we say, do, wear, drive, matters. Our personal brand is not the professional head shot on a blog or social media profile, but the total effect of everything we put out there. The implications are huge." (Maurilio Amorim) [13]

As Christian leaders in the marketplace, the implications are huge as Paul reminds us in 2 Corinthians 3:2-3 (Good News Translation GN) "*You yourselves are the letter.... for everyone to know and read. It is written not with ink but with the Spirit of the living God...*" It is regrettable that too often people live one way when the spotlights are on and another way behind closed doors. Credibility answers this critical question – what are you really like when no one is looking? May I respectfully submit, that the world is beset by too many fake and unauthentic brands, while it is true for marketing, it is also true of leadership today. We need to set a different standard informed by a different set of values.

We are living in a society that is obsessed with image. There is an entire global industry out there today, created around image consulting, reputation management, influencers, and the like. When I speak about credibility as being the DNA of your personal brand, I am referring to those innate qualities that define who you are. Those intangibles, sometimes referred to as brand essence that gives people a good feel about you. It is about an appreciation of the uniqueness of your personal identity, not being a copy of somebody else and knows exactly what values you represent. Once you have come to terms with these aspects, you will be able to connect with your target market and evoke real and meaningful responses.

You are the brand!

Learn it. Live it. Lead it!

How to develop credibility

Credibility is not accomplished through a singular event but develops over a period of time. It is aspirational but should be approached with a high degree of intentionality. My car came out with a Motorplan scheme which guarantees free repairs and maintenance expenses whilst the car is under warranty. However, this offer is only valid if I stick to the prescribed service schedule and comply with the prescripts of the Motorplan. Failing to do so, will cause the warranty to be rendered invalid. It is the same with credibility, it needs to be diligently maintained otherwise we can so easily lose it. We need to develop a strong sense of self-awareness whereby we become honest and keep our credibility intact.

The first submission that any bright or successful leader needs to understand concerning credibility is:

- No title is big enough to impose it.
- It does not emerge from a corner office.
- The level on which your car and its model is parked is inconsequential.
- Perks and salary can be misleading.

It is fragile and should therefore be handled with the utmost care. How do you think a leader of significance must feel though walking a straight line and uncompromising in his or her dealings with others, when several disgruntled union members totally destabilise the working environment and demand his or her resignation? Leadership then becomes vulnerable enough to appreciate that my credibility is in the eye of the beholder. Though it is not always totally within my power, but I am always going to give it my best shot.

The second submission I would like to make is that whenever I assume a leadership position, I am mindful that three unanswered questions will always linger in the minds of my team, who by the way might also verbalize answers, even if unsolicited. These three questions must all be answered in the affirmative and our answers should be sufficiently convincing:

1. In which way is the leader like me? Is he a man or woman amongst other men or women or vice-versa?
2. Does he or she know what he or she is talking about?
3. What track record of success is he or she bringing along?

The third submission is, if credibility is not totally in his or her power, what is? What inspires absolute confidence? I would like to suggest the following borne out of my own experience:

- When team members "look over your shoulders" at what you say, write or do, is there gratifying evidence of forethought? Are you ahead of the idea curve? Have you been to the "mountain" to inspire confidence about your ability to take a calculated risk? Do you anticipate hurdles and obstacles before it hits you or the organisation you are leading?
- Do you cause things to happen? Do you inspire the team that you have at a personal level, what it would take to deliver? Are you a "can make it happen" functionary?
- Do you bounce back to display a comeback after a setback? Resilience is going to be one of your critic's strongest barometers.

During my journey in the top echelons of the corporate environment, it always baffled me how many institutions suffer from the type of leader who cannot see beyond his or her own path to the top. They were great operational managers, legal heads, finance officers etc. but when the C-suit opened, they battle to transition to a role that warrants a more strategic approach. They cannot resist the temptation of veering back to their operational default position and in the process disempower those that are now responsible for that domain. The downside is that their primary area of responsibility is starved of strategic input.

I have interviewed many candidates for senior management positions on my leadership journey. One of the interviews that I will never forget was when we interviewed a candidate for a General Manager's position in the Electrotechnical Division of SABS. There was a candidate by the name of Ronald, who was a qualified electrical engineer and had just recently completed his master's degree in business administration (MBA). We kicked off with the normal questions about why he applied and what learning experiences prepared him for the respective role. Quite early in the interview after going through some of the introductory stuff, Ronald flipped the interview right on its head and raised a question directly to me as the CEO of the company. He asked me very respectfully yet in a pointed manner – Mr Kuscus tell me how did you become CEO of SABS? As he raised his question, I could sense a bit of tension on the side of my fellow panellists. I answered him as comprehensively as possible and really enjoyed the interaction as he raised follow-up questions. At our debriefing session when my colleagues described him as a bit arrogant, I told them I saw a visionary. This young engineer knew what he wanted out of life and was not prepared to mortgage his future to a leader who did not have the capability to assist him in getting there. He wanted to know exactly how long it would take and what it would take to become my successor. Today's emerging leaders will only subject themselves to the authority of leaders that are credible; those that could value their potential and develop it to the maximum. If you fit the bill, their loyalty and diligence will be unsurpassed and benefit the overall organisational performance.

Leadership is such a powerful yet vulnerable space. The one moment you can inspire people to accomplish the impossible in pursuit of the common good and the next there is the potential to do irreversible harm to people if there is an error of judgement on your side. At the heart of credibility lies the issue of trust. Trust is indispensable for a relationship to succeed. In a marriage relationship you need to have trust and confidence in your partner to honour the marriage vows even in your absence and not engage in any act that will compromise the integrity of the union. When it comes to finances, you need to have trust in your financial advisor to deploy your money in a manner that yields the expected returns and not help him or herself at your expense. As business partners, there should be absolute trust that all your efforts will be directed to co-create a thriving enterprise without one of the partners secretly running a side show at the expense of the business. Being in a position of leadership demands a higher level of trust because you carry the hopes, aspirations, and dreams of those you are leading.

I read quite an insightful article recently by Hal Seed on the Three Unspoken Promises people expect their leaders to keep.[14] Within this unwritten and unspoken exchange, is a covenant, agreement, contract, undertaking or pledge that all leaders make to their followers when they sign up for the cause. This unspoken covenant contains three promises:

1. If you follow me, I will make your life better.
2. If you follow me, I will care about you.
3. If you follow me, I will take you where you cannot go on your own.

These are very profound statements that we all as leaders ought to heed and endeavour to deliver on in an honest and consistent manner, lest we unleash the wrath of those at whose behest we are leading. It also makes us vigilant and instils in us a greater sense of responsibility that it is not about prestige, status or how well we can spin the facts. Leadership is all about stewardship and servanthood, prioritising concern for the destiny of others above our own.

In the next few chapters I would like to focus in more detail on eight aspects which in my leadership journey, had greatly assisted in building my credibility as a leader.

PART B – HOW TO DEVELOP CREDIBILITY

Chapter 4

UNCOMPROMISING CHARACTER

Character refers to the totality of a person's distinct qualities both good and bad, that translates into how that person expresses him or herself in any given setting. Character is not some ritual that is drilled into you to be performed at a designated time and opportunity, but it is a matter of inner reality. Character answers this critical question – what are you really like when no one is looking?

Character is therefore an indispensable building block in developing your credibility. Let me also hasten to say that it comes at a high premium. Likewise, there is also a high price to pay for low living. The key driver in low living is compromise; the expedient acceptance of standards that are lower than the desirable. If we settle for lower standards, it can have serious consequences for our future well-being and our mission in life will never be fulfilled. That cheap lie, malicious gossip, selfishness, taking a brown envelope underneath the table, not following through with the promises you have made, the casual fling with someone from the opposite sex, allowing yourself to be used for the nefarious agendas of others, unsubstantiated prejudice and discrimination and being lukewarm in matters of faith, will progressively shape your character with devastating consequences.

The most profound definition I read about character is the one of David Stoddard:

"Character is what is left after the fire." [15] What he is simply trying to say is that character is the ultimate proof of who you really are after being tested and refined by the experiences of life, both good and bad. When your back is against the wall, it will reveal what is in the inside of you. Likewise, when you are wallowing in abundance and everything you put your hand on seems to turn into gold, it will equally reveal what is on the inside of you.

The world thrives on compromise where people are prepared to sell their souls in pursuit of selfish ambitions. Truth has become a relative concept in our day and age; everything is rationalised depending on the context. One can at times be so desperate to seek approval and try to fit in with the crowds, that you will be prepared to "look the other way" on issues of principle. This can become such a hollow experience because you are not truthful to yourself. While pursuing a good name and reputation, there is a strong likelihood of being criticised, rejected, misunderstood, wilfully sabotaged and even being exposed to harm by those who have set their minds on low standards and get irritated by your superior approach to life. This is not about adopting a holier than thou kind of attitude but a genuine and sincere attempt to live your best life possible.

We have been created in the image and likeness of God. We therefore need to represent Him well in all our endeavours. Never compromise on your faith. All our thoughts, actions and attitudes should conform to the standards of God's Word. We will be well advised to acquaint ourselves daily with the letter and spirit of its contents. Any neglect in this regard, will draw us into the realm of cheap and low living.

Never compromise on your family life; it can have generational implications. What we model to our children in our homes, will greatly shape their outlook towards life. Never compromise in our marriage relationships. The consequence of infidelity can be devastating and costly. I am intensely aware that marriage and family life is not an easy ride, but we should never forget that it is established on a covenant relationship. During the Covid -19 pandemic, I once more developed a fresh appreciation for the good fortune of having one another in holy matrimony and the awareness that at any moment, life could take one of us away. We cannot therefore waste our time in low living but instead invest time to create enduring memories.

"Truth doesn't grow grey with time. But moral eyes can become dimmed by cataracts of compromise." John Bloom. [16]

There is a high price to pay for not upholding an uncompromising character. It comes with a lot of regrets, guilt, shame, disillusionment, and unfulfilled potential. Let us live a qualitative life of moral rectitude, having a sincere desire to always do the right things for the right reasons. The rewards are so fulfilling, and we will continue to grow instead of stagnating; we will glorify God and earn the respect of others.

One can feel so overwhelmed at times when constantly bombarded with news about corrupt practices and impropriety. Recently I read the words spoken by the Lord to Elijah at the height of his despondency when confronted with the level of moral decay in the nation. *"Yet I reserved 7000 in Israel; all whose knees have not bowed to Baal and whose mouths have not kissed him."* 1 Kings 19:18 (NKJV) These profound words are still as relevant today as they were written.

Daily we observe some very disturbing incidences where there is a conscious and deliberate disregard for sound values. Like Elijah, you and I might sometimes feel alone in our struggle against this raging tide. It is however comforting to know that there are still 7000 in Israel who have not bowed their knees to Baal. Regrettably, there are just as many leaders in the marketplace that have bowed to the idols of power, materialism, and fame; having fallen in love with the false sense of security and identity accorded by it. Billy Graham once said: *"It is not about possession but obsession."* [17] Lurking at the heart of it all, is the spirit of greed. Hence the escalation in economic crime as reported earlier, manifesting itself in a culture of endemic corruption that became a way of life in the marketplace.

Living a life of sound character, is a matter of choice. I found the guidelines regarding decision making of Raymond Hillgert in his book Christian Ethics in the Workplace, quite instructive. He cites the following: [18]

- Am I operating within the limits of the law?
- How would the broader public react to my decision?

- What are the long-term consequences of my decision?
- Are my motives pure and for the benefit of others and the organization?
- Do I have a clear conscience about my decision?

It is my fervent desire that we shall rise to the challenge and make a firm commitment at an individual and corporate level to say "No" to corruption. I am mindful of the fact that there is a price to be paid for being honest, making a special effort to keep your word, going against popular opinion and owning up for your mistakes.

Are you one amongst the 7000?

You are as good as the company you keep

Your character is greatly shaped by the company you keep. Someone once said – show me your friends and I will show you your destiny. One of my friends Maurice Radebe turned 60 towards the end of 2020 and is now officially on retirement. His family commissioned a video about his life thus far and requested me to make an input about our journey and the impact he made on my life. After the crew filmed the interview at my house, I was preoccupied with one question after they left. "Besides my wife, who are my friends?"

As we grow older, meaningful friendships become very tough to maintain. In my school days, friends were never in short supply. Even as a teenager and during early adulthood, I was quite a likeable fellow and could easily connect with people. As the years progressed, life got busy. There were work, family and career advancement goals that were competing with my ability to cultivate and expand my circle of friendship. Another complicating factor as I moved on in my years, is the lurking possibility of betrayal. I am sure if I ask you when was the last time that you were let down by a friend, being misunderstood or simply just ignored; I would not be surprised if it happened last week, last month or even last year. That is simply the reality of life. Our repetitive exposure to such incidences can subtly lead to a sense of withdrawal from friendships because we do not want to take risks anymore. We are also living in such a highly competitive world where everyone seems to be embarking on manoeuvres to outsmart one another. Therefore, it becomes rather difficult to be transparent and open to one another out of fear that someone will use the personal information conveyed in confidence and use it to his/ her advantage.

Notwithstanding all the contradictions, I am fully convinced that friendships matter. There is however an important element about building enduring friendships as described by Gordon MacDonald *"Friendships don't just happen. They are developed and they are maintained. They are not accidental and self-perpetuating. They must be cultivated much as a plant is carefully developed from seed to blossom."* [19] It is in the crucible of authentic friendships where character is shaped.

The following aspects are particularly important to cultivate healthy friendships:

- Clarify values: Values are those matters that are not negotiable, that inform important behaviour in your life. All endeavours are then calibrated against these values. If there is a misalignment of values in a friendship, it is bound to be a real source of unhappiness.
- Be intentional: Friendship is about a conscious and deliberate choice to journey with someone. It is being mindful that it is not going to be smooth sailing all the time. It requires a positive mind-set where you always see the best in your friend, choosing to serve selflessly and affirms progress registered. It is also about having an open and accommodative attitude and extending forgiveness when the friendship goes through a rough patch.
- Authenticity: This is the hallmark of healthy friendships. If you veered from the agreed principles that you have committed to, own up for your mistakes. We all have the potential to disappoint one another. Lies, deceit, defensiveness and cover ups undermine any friendship.
- Teachability: When I depart from any engagement with a friend, I need to be able to respond positively to the question, "What lesson have I learned from this interaction?" I am on a continuous growth path and appreciate encounters that stretch my mind. Good friends are good listeners.

- Have fun: I need to look forward to being with my friends as a necessary strategic diversion from the pressure cooker environment of other facets of my life. Doing fun things together helps to recharge and unwind, builds and contributes to our photo album of long-lasting memories. There are three guiding principles when having fun: Know your play mates. Know your playground. Know your playthings.

I can without a shadow of a doubt testify that my character has been greatly shaped by strategic friendships that came across my path. Solomon said in Proverbs 13: 20 (MSG) *"Become wise by walking with the wise; hang out with fools and watch your life fall to pieces."* I will always be grateful for the privilege of journeying with a handful of men who I really regard as true friends. I do not know how I would have made it thus far especially now through the Covid-19 pandemic without their loyal support, thoughtfulness, accountability, and objective feedback. It challenged me afresh to cultivate and maintain true friendships. It is an invaluable part for my character development.

Friendship matters. Who are your friends?

It is time to go to the lab

I spent about five years of my life in the quality industry as CEO of the South African Bureau of Standards. It is no secret that billions are lost in trade opportunities because unscrupulous operators dump inferior products on their domestic market. Some of them brazenly export it to other countries where enforcement of trade regulations is weak. This poses a tremendous risk to the health and safety of the consumer.

A key differentiator that can give a high degree of comfort to a consumer, is the whole aspect of quality. It has become international best practice to subject a product or service to an independent third-party verification process by doing specific tests, assessments, or inspections on it. If the product or service is found to meet all the standards and specifications, it is then formally approved and issued with a quality certificate, signifying that it is fit for purpose.

From a leadership perspective, it is regrettable and heart - wrenching that some of us who are paraded as leaders, have not gone through the rigor of quality assurance. We are sometimes prematurely launched into a position of authority without having been certified as fit for purpose. It should therefore not come as a surprise that when some leaders are exposed to the real challenges of leadership, their fault lines are badly exposed. Even on matters of character, if the foundation is brittle and not based on strong principles, the cracks will show in your life, and you will not be able to stand indefinitely.

The ultimate standard to which all our endeavours in life and especially in leadership needs to conform, is the word of God. In 2 Timothy 3:16-17 (MSG) Paul states it as follows: "*All scripture is inspired by God and is useful one way or another – showing us truth, exposing our rebellion, correcting our mistakes, training us to live God's way. Through the Word we are put together and shaped up for the tasks God has for us.*"

Whilst being at the SABS, it always fascinated me when I did laboratory rounds, how some of the ordinary goods we use, are subjected to such a strenuous and rigorous test regime. I would just like to highlight the following tests and its application for qualitative leadership:

1. Endurance test

Certain products for example solar heater panels, are subjected over an extended period, to various climatic conditions to test their level of endurance under these conditions. Likewise, as a leader you must demonstrate strength to persevere in difficult circumstances. Gordon Mac Donald in his book A Resilient Life states "*Resilient people train to go the distance. They keep themselves physically fit; grow their minds; harness their emotions and trim their egos.*"[20]

2. Chemical test

In chemistry, we test the minute constituents that the substance is made of and how it reacts when another chemical is introduced into the specimen. In leadership we also need to maintain our original composition. Too many of us want to conform to be accepted. We have not been called to conform but to remain truthful to our character in whatever environment we find ourselves. Remain stable and settled in your soul.

3. Waiting test

Some test results can only be validated over an extended period and through a few repetitions over a few cycles for example drug trials. We are living in the microwave millennium, an instant age where leaders sometimes fall into the trap of quick fixes and instant results. There comes a time in the life of a leader where your patience will be tested and waiting becomes a taxing proposition and at times a bit untenable. Delay is not denial. Take heart, God's timing is always on schedule.

4. Isolation test

Certain tests are performed in very obscure circumstances with minimal human intervention. A leader also needs to appreciate that loneliness is part of the leadership package. There will come a time in a leader's life where he or she feels totally separated from others. If you cannot handle loneliness and love playing to the gallery, stay out of leadership. Leadership is almost like conducting an orchestra, you need to give your back to the audience and focus on the execution of the musical performance. It is only after the task has been completed successfully, then you can turn to the audience and take a bow. You are not running a fan club when you are into a serious leadership assignment. There is loneliness of decision making, confidentiality and just the awesome realization that the buck stops with you.

5. Performance test

When a product or system is tested, it must be able to perform at the required specification or yield the results as expected. I always marvelled at how a seatbelt test is run over and over with a dummy passenger sometimes for days because it is a mission critical part of a vehicle. In leadership, we are also responsible to deliver the goods as dictated by the demands at that time. Indecision, procrastination, and the inability to follow-through, can have a detrimental effect on performance.

Consumers normally use very derogatory names when speaking about fake and inferior products. To maintain the necessary respect and dignity of the office we occupy, let us maintain the highest level of qualitative leadership. Quality is not a once-off event but a continuous process. When last have you been in the laboratory subjecting yourself to the appropriate verification processes? If done regularly, it will ensure that you are calibrated for optimal performance, you maintain your character and your leadership actions will not become a risk to the health and safety of your organization. Subjecting your character frequently to quality assurance processes is a key differentiator that will enable you to stay course on.

Frank Otlaw puts the importance of character formation so aptly:

> *"Watch your thoughts, they become words.*
> *Watch your words, they become actions.*
> *Watch your actions, they become habits.*
> *Watch your habits, they become character.*
> *Watch your character because it becomes your destiny."* [21]

PITSTOP

In 1996 while I was MEC of Finance in the North West Province, I was appointed in an additional portfolio of Economic Affairs. By that time, the issuing of casino licences was a hot topic in South Africa, and this ended up being under my portfolio. It was really a challenging task because just for the record, I abhor gambling, but I had a job to fulfil and could not allow my objectivity to be clouded in this regard. I became hot property and was forever invited to gala events, golf days (I had just started to play by then) and all manner of invitations to luxury game farms and the like. All invitations triggered in me some conspiratorial response and I instinctively declined them. What I did however not seen coming, was an invitation by a well-known businessman in my hometown of Klerksdorp to discuss some socio-economic proposal for the community.

I was scheduled to attend a funeral in Alabama one Saturday of one of my former teachers. On my way there, I met this businessman on his farm on the outskirts of Klerksdorp. He drove me on a short tour of his farm, to soak up the scenic surroundings. We finally settled down and his wife served us with some hot scones fresh from the oven and nice tea. My guest ultimately brokered the subject, and I was surprised how well he knew government's policy by then known as the Reconstruction and Development Programme (RDP) as he engaged me. What was however shocking, was when he relegated the noble ideals of the RDP, to a very direct request for me to secure him a casino licence. The farm would purportedly be turned into a big money-spinning resort. It will supposedly bring much needed jobs and economic activity to my hometown which was experiencing a slump in job opportunities due to a downturn in the gold mining industry. But it did not end there. He made me aware of how well he was connected to some ministers from the previous regime. The lesson he wanted me to understand was that I should look out for myself whilst in politics because it had a limited shelf life. He proposed setting up a blind trust fund and promised to water the tree with the proceeds. When I exited politics, it would be a nice big tree for me to access the fruits.

I was listening very attentively to this guy who spoke with so much enthusiasm about his proposal. Now these were still early days in my political career; no balance sheet to write home about and the unpredictability of politics. But by that time I was so focussed, enjoying this new political responsibility and going about it with a high degree of integrity. Suffice to say, the conversation did not last that long and I only enjoyed one scone. I laid out the envisaged official process to him and in a very polite manner told him unequivocally that this tree planting business is not my scene and proceeded to the funeral.

Lessons learned:

1. I had to remind myself constantly that politics was not just a job to me but a calling to serve the wellbeing of the people of the North West and above all, to glorify God in everything I do.

2. Anything could have gone wrong in this so-called blind trust arrangement and where funny money is involved, the ugliness of a human being usually comes to the fore.
3. If I succumbed to that proposition, I would not have been favoured by God to be exposed to the GEPF, SABS, United Nations, ISO, JSE and all these other life-changing opportunities. This test gave me a testimony whereby I gained the respect in the marketplace and God was glorified in my endeavours. Over the years, God used me to minister with great impact in many conferences and high impact meetings to leaders about my testimony and how to live out your faith in the marketplace. I might have been sitting on my back porch, if things went wrong with this proposition and reflecting on this perennial question- if only?

What are you really like when no one is looking?

Chapter 5

ABSOLUTE CLARITY OF DIRECTION

How many of us are cruising along the journey of life merely going through the motions? We have put in all the hard miles to get what we so much wanted; money, titles, material abundance, a high public profile, only to discover that it is not what you thought it would be. We are just cruising along wondering whether things might have been different. If only God had given us the full download about His plan and purpose for our lives without any hassles. Well, we know that this is not how real life operates.

To develop meaning in your life, you must have a vision. I am referring here to that compelling picture that you constantly need to have in your mind of what a preferred future would look like; spurring you on to excel. As much as vision is there to motivate, it also acts as guardrails and instil in us a sense of discipline to keep us on track. One of the most important aspects about vision, is that it should always be about a higher purpose. The revered Helen Keller made this profound statement about the importance of vision "The *only thing worse than being blind is having sight but no vision.*"[22]

We have seen at this point in time in the history of humanity, how people are looking up to leaders for clarity as we navigate uncharted territory. It is not always possible to provide those you are leading with absolute certainty about the outcome of a sequence of events. There are sometimes variables at play over which the leader simply has no control. The least that people expect from their leaders, is a sense of clarity on the course of action to be undertaken. This warrants that the leader should have a clear vision. It is important for Godly leaders to have a vision of the future that God destined for us. The relentless pursuit of vision gives you credibility. The wise king Solomon once said in Proverbs 29:18 (King James Version KJV) "*Where there is no vision, the people perish.*" Conversely, I would like to submit to you that where there is vision, the people flourish. Too many leaders lose their credibility because everything excites them. They jump from one project to the other with a great deal of fanfare but when you check their track record, there is nothing of substance to show and their big talk did not match up with any results at all.

We therefore need to prayerfully spend time and effort in understanding how to draw one's intentions and desires out of the deep reservoirs of your heart to the surface, so that it make sense to be practically implemented. This all starts with the critical process of envisioning. It is about looking beyond the immediate into the distant future.

It is one thing to have a compelling picture about a desired future, it should however be translated into tangible reality. The following are key aspects that will assist in keeping your vision on track:

- Write it down. I was so encouraged when I read Habakkuk 2: 2 -3 (Contemporary English Version CEV) the other day "*Then the Lord told me: I will give you my message in the form of a vision. Write it clearly enough to be read at a glance. At the time that I have decided, my words will come true. You can trust what I say about the future. It may take a long time but keep on waiting – it will happen.*"

  Once you have clarity on what the end picture should look like, write it out in a manner that is simple, powerful, with passion and energy. If reading it does not excite you, it is very unlikely to set the world alight.
- Create a plan for your vision. The adage – failing to plan is planning to fail, cannot be overemphasised. Make a proper assessment of what resources need to be mobilised to make it happen. Also factor

in what sacrifices you will have to make for the vision to become a reality.

- Act on the plan. If you do not act on your vision, it will just remain a nice slogan of intent. Pastor Ray McCauley made quite a profound statement earlier this year in one of his sermons that really excited me "*Effective people know that you do not have to be great to start but start to be great.*"
- Create systems and processes that will act as enablers to make implementation possible.
- Authentic feedback. Have a few key people in your life that can act as an accountability structure from whom you can solicit authentic feedback.

At the beginning of 2021, while reflecting on the way ahead, I was strongly challenged by John 15 of which verse 16 seemed to "jump of the page" and greatly shaped my direction for the year. It states "*You did not choose me, but I chose you and appointed you so that you might go and bear fruit – fruit that will last – and so that whatever you ask in my name the Father will give you.*" (New International Version NIV). The directive to me is abundantly clear – "Appointed to Bear Fruit that will last." My whole destiny revolves around this directive. This brought into focus a few key questions that I had to grapple with, some of which are:

- Am I making maximum impact in my family, business roles, church, and community in what I have been called to do?
- What am I going to build my life around to bear fruit that will last?

Our purpose in life, is a progressive revelation as we grow in our relationship with God. It is a matter of trust. Although I might not know the full details, I trust and believe wholeheartedly that He always has my best interest at heart. Harsh tests await us on our journey, but this is meant to deepen our own understanding of who God intended us to be. Our dependence on God is enhanced as we seek Him continuously in all our endeavours, so that when we are released into our purpose, we will know who made it possible. It also sensitises us to our need for interdependence. No person of significance in life, made it without the influence and support of others.

I thank God for the promise "*... whatever you ask in my name the Father will give you.*" Do you need wisdom, strength, courage, provision...? Whatever is needed in our envisioning process and its implementation, will be given if we abide in the vine and remain faithful to our calling.

Never allow your current reality to define who you really are

It is no secret; we all yearn to be loved by others. It is however a fact of life that wherever there is human interaction, there is always the possibility that people will have differences of opinion, disliking one another and sometimes just outright jealousy and envy for reasons best known to the perpetrator. Some of these tendencies can become so mean and inhumane that it can even create doubt in your mind about your identity. Surprisingly, some of these opinions may come from those least expected; those doing life side by side with us in our families, workplaces, community organisations, congregants and even those regarded as close friends. If the message of failure, not having the right credentials and hopelessness is repeatedly reinforced, it can have a detrimental effect on our approach towards life, our vision, sense of purpose and meaning.

Another critical factor that can have a major influence on our lives, is the environment in which socialization takes place. The environment can have a positive influence on people's behaviour and can facilitate meaningful interactions towards the common good. Conversely, the environment can be a serious impediment towards optimisation of potential. Given some of our unfortunate history as a country, many of our people come from very disadvantaged backgrounds, having survived tough and impoverished conditions. We had no choice in where we were brought up. Orison Marden describes it this way "*Your outlook of life, your estimate of yourself and your estimate of your value are largely coloured by your environment.*"[23]

Allow me to share with you the words of some of the following luminaries who did not allow their current reality to define who they really are:

"I did not even complete my university education but became one of the world's richest men." Bill Gates

"I was raped at the age of 9 yet I am one of the most influential women in the world." Oprah Winfrey

"I used to serve tea at a shop to support my football training and today I am one of the world's best football players." Lionel Messi

"I struggled academically throughout elementary school yet became the best neurosurgeon in the world in 1987." Dr Ben Carson

"I was in prison for 27 years and still became president of my country." Nelson Mandela

"I was sexually, mentally, emotionally abused by my father as far back as I can remember until I left home at the age of 18. Yet, today I am one of the most influential preachers in the world." Joyce Meyer

"I used to sleep on the floor of my friends' rooms, returning Coke bottles for food money and getting weekly free meals at a local temple. I later on founded one of the world's biggest brands, the Apple Company." Steve Jobs

"I started Living Faith Church from a Lawn Tennis Court with only three members. Many of my friends criticised me but today we have the largest church auditorium in the world and two world class universities." Bishop David Oyedepo [24]

It is quite clear from the above examples that these individuals did not allow setbacks, constraints, and disappointments to determine their self-worth and stop them from fulfilling their vision and purpose in life.

People's opinions, no matter how uncomfortable it might have been at times, did not change who they really were. Even if you fail and miss the mark, stand up, dust yourself off and move forward in pursuit of your vision in life. Move forward to keep the vision alive. Love again, serve again, laugh again, and walk in faith again. You see when you constantly blame others, you give them a licence to control your destiny. Do not allow others to define you, define your own life through a well - considered vision.

I have done a bit of research on most of the men and women listed above and was astounded by their great sense of generosity. If one thinks for example of the millions of dollars the Bill Gates Foundation gives away every year to tackle the challenges of poverty, disease, and inequality on a global scale. These people have learned that it is about using their resources and influence to touch the lives of others. You and I might not be billionaires or high-profile figures in world affairs, but we need to work towards meaning and purpose in our small sphere of influence. We need to define for ourselves, how our mission in life can contribute towards the well-being of others in a practical way. It will free us up from the notion to prove something and safeguard us from the trappings of greed and selfishness.

Marshall Segal sums it up so beautifully *"Wherever we work, we've been deployed by God as agents of everlasting joy."* [25] Whose life will I touch today? What challenges am I going to turn around into wealth creating opportunities? Which obstacles am I going to embrace as part of learning and development? Never allow your current reality to define who you are. There is a bigger picture at play here; far above what you have ever thought, prayed, or imagined.

The road towards accomplishing a great vision, is a lonely one

From a distance, people always marvel at the glamour, glitz and attention that is sometimes accorded to people in influential positions. It seems that leaders unknowingly attract interest and respect that will cause people to instinctively give anything to be in the company of the leader they hold in high esteem. Every word spoken, any initiative launched, any social activity or whatever the leader gets him or herself involved with, becomes a point of reference and often a benchmark to be emulated. There is however a part that is not frequently being spoken of and that is the uncomfortable reality of leadership called loneliness.

Far removed from the glare of spotlights and public attention, many leaders can sometimes feel a sense of intense loneliness. The loneliness comes from the realisation of the awesome responsibility that rests upon him or her in pursuit of a great vision and the potential consequences of every action or inaction. There will come a time when the applause of the crowds fades into deafening silence. You will become even conspiratorial at times about the motives of those close to you and even believing in yourself becomes an arduous assignment. The greater the vision, the greater the likelihood of loneliness. Just be mindful that a Godly vision does not happen on a big conference call, it is ultimately a personal assignment between you and God.

David Mc Kenna in his book Never Blink at a Hailstorm [26] describes the following three types of loneliness in leadership which greatly assisted in my own moments of loneliness during my respective leadership assignments:

1. The loneliness of authority: You might experience isolation in exercising authority especially in correcting a wrong that became a norm in your organisation. Some of your closest associates might not necessarily like the status quo to be challenged.
2. The loneliness of decision making: Leaders sometimes grapple with decisions that can have far reaching implications. The mere realisation that the buck stops with you, can be quite daunting.
3. The loneliness of confidentiality: There are sometimes moral dilemmas that leaders must deal with where integrity of the institution, an individual or a family is at stake. Are you going to make a public case that will send shock waves through the organisation or are you going to take the route of rehabilitation and confidentiality without compromising accountability?

On my leadership journey, I have been challenged on all three fronts on numerous occasions. Sometimes it happened at the peak of executing an exciting vision. Most of the times there were no textbook answers or precedents from which to reference. I always draw great inspiration from the life of Jesus Christ who was arguably the greatest leader ever that graced the face of the earth. During His crucifixion all the disciples except one deserted Him, to the point where He even cried out in Mark 15: 34 (NKJV) *"My God, my God, why has thou forsaken me?"* Since He knows the depths of loneliness, He is willing and able to strengthen and guide me in my moments of uncomfortable loneliness. He promised in His Word that He will never leave me or forsake me. This rings true as heralded by my favourite soccer team Liverpool's anthem "You never walk alone."

I am sure that in your life as in mine, there were times whilst embarking on a great vision, you also went through moments of uncertainty that engendered a sense of uncomfortable loneliness. This might include severing ties with a long- standing business partner because of impropriety, recapitalising a business, confronting a very senior colleague who was disrupting organisational objectives, serious unforeseen and unavoidable cost escalations where money is in short supply etc.

There will be times which seems as if you are between a rock and a hard place. If you find yourself in such uncertain circumstances:

- Know who you are and what your assignment in life is all about.
- Develop an appropriate mental attitude. As Martin Gover once said, *"Attitude is 100% under your control; yours to choose, use or lose."* [27]
- Live today as if it is your last. Living a life that pleases God should be foremost in your mind. Forget yesterday's setbacks and the potential challenges of tomorrow. Embrace today and give it your best shot.
- Never forget that there are people's lives that depend on the successful implementation of the vision. They really care about you and there is more going for you then what is against you.

You are the custodian of a vision much bigger than yourself. Engage the uncomfortable reality of loneliness, with hope.

A few months ago, I received a message that really caused me to reflect deeply about the investments that I endeavour to make into the lives of others. It reinforces the importance of getting clarity of direction in one's life. When I was still living in Mafikeng, I was invited by the late Pastor Amos Dladla who was running a prison ministry at Rooigrond Prison on Sundays, to come and motivate the prisoners at their year-end function. I gave a brief testimony of myself and the journey that the Lord had brought me through. I then anchored the rest of my input around having a vision for your life. I reminded the prisoners that they are not defined by their current reality but whilst incarcerated, they needed to start visualising a picture about a preferred future when released from prison. There was quite an encouraging response when I made an altar call.

Now after many years a gentleman by the name of Fani, ultimately tracked me down on one of the social media platforms and he dropped me the following note:

"Good morning Mr Kuscus. Just to let you know that your ministry at Rooigrond Prison in the late 90's, has impacted my life profoundly. I was released in the year 2005 and my life improved tremendously. I am a husband, father and community leader today. Got my BA degree and am now doing skills development in corporates. I remember the sermon you preached entitled – Who are you? What do you say about yourself? It was through that sermon whereby the Lord God Almighty led me into a journey of rediscovering my identity. I really appreciate the investment that God has made in my life through your ministry!" What more can I say? One cannot derive any greater satisfaction in life then knowing you have impacted someone's life for the better.

Our credibility is greatly influenced by our ability to pursue a compelling vision. Without a compelling vision we will just be drifting and floating around; nobody will take us seriously. When we pursue the right vision for our lives, we not only gain the respect of others, but God gets glorified through our endeavours.

PITSTOP

One of the defining moments in my life was to read the book of Bob Buford called *Halftime* in 2009. The central theme of the book is how to translate your success into significance. Many people like myself, who had quite successful careers in the first half of their lives, are increasingly searching for the answer to these pressing questions "Is there more to life than my current situation?" "What can I do to make my life to count for something more fulfilling, more meaningful and more eternally significant?" I was so absorbed in the book's contents for weeks and it triggered a deep desire in me to transition from what I regarded as an extraordinarily successful life by then, to a life of significance.

We all have been in a stage of life where it almost sounded too good to be true. You may be a rising star and riding on the crest of the wave. However, you may become disinterested in your current environment and the question might even have crossed your mind, "What's wrong with me?"

In my case there was this healthy anxiety, longing for something but not knowing what it was. It felt as I had been in an emotional wilderness where the things that defined my identity, purpose and security became meaningless. I came from a period of exceptional success in my career and it seemed as if there was a sudden withdrawal of the adrenaline that drove me. As I went through the book, there developed in me a deep longing to leave behind an enduring legacy. It was this thought-provoking statement that really caught my attention: *"One of the most common characteristics of a person who is nearing the end of his first half, is that unquenchable desire to move from success to significance. After a first half of doing what we are supposed to do, we would like to do something in the second half that is more meaningful – something that rises above perks and pay-checks into the stratosphere of significance."* (Bob Buford) [28]

I recall one afternoon while on a business trip in Tasmania, I was sitting at a very cosy coffee shop with Liz. My contract at SABS was about to expire within five months and we were just reflecting on the prospects of moving forward. I still remember taking out a sheet of paper and gave Liz a diagrammatical explanation about my envisaged "Half Time" journey.

After listening very attentively to my initial thoughts about transitioning from success to significance, her response was quite profound. She said that she would back me all the way on the journey but that there is one missing piece in the whole equation and that was her need for stability. We were in our fifties and the margin of error was exceedingly small. I took note of this very real concern in all my endeavours as I moved forward. I made well calculated moves mindful not to compromise the stability of our family life. As a matter of fact, we grew much closer ever since and are really enjoying our lives in what is now the empty nest phase of our family life.

The desire for significance never escaped me and I ultimately located a local coach from the Halftime Institute, Mathilda Fourie at the end of 2012 and enrolled for their programme. I was joined by three other business executives on a nine-month journey. It was life defining and greatly assisted me in responding appropriately to my desire for significance. I came to the realisation that if I do not reinvent myself, life would go into a downward spiral. I had to leverage from my past life experiences to maintain an upward momentum.

Our group met once per month for a half-day session on Saturdays and then we had to work through a lot of practical yet soul searching stuff throughout the month. Very early on in these encounters, I discovered that it was more a of a heart journey than that of the head. There are five areas in which a transformation of my heart occurred:

1. My journey to a new identity. In the past my identity was defined by the titles and positions I occupied. I had to honestly reflect on what truths about me, would define my new identity.
2. The development of new performance standards. I was very performance driven although there is absolutely nothing wrong with performance per se. Living a life of eternal significance might sometimes be difficult to measure in the short term.
3. I discovered the strength of interdependence. I realised that what we can offer together is more than the sum of what we could offer independently.

4. Finding a new longing for intimacy. I was so busy and got caught up in the pace and pursuit of my goals that I did not give sufficient time to understand the value of intimacy or dismantle the barriers that stood in the way of enjoying maximum intimacy with my Creator.
5. Seeing the hero in being a servant. I now find much deeper satisfaction in life pursuing significance as a servant.

One of the spiritual disciplines that was instilled in us, was to go on monthly Solo Retreats. It is a day or sometimes two, in which you totally unplug from your mobile phone, emails, television and the news. It is during these Solo Retreats that I also had to seek God's direction to craft a mission statement for the second half of my life.

After various iterations informed by prayer and solitude as well as the guidance of my coach and fellow team members, I got clear confirmation about what would inform my journey moving forward. To sum it up in one sentence – *Martin will be a thought leader, developing Christian leaders in the marketplace for Kingdom impact.*

The next phase of the journey was to work out the context in which this mission was going to be realised. My core strengths are strategy, people development and communication. I also had to consider what capacity I need to deploy to leverage from my strengths and gain momentum. Through God's grace I started to live out this mission in the following areas:

- I serve as Chairperson on the South African Board of Lead Like Jesus and has been part of the movement for the past seven years. We have been doing encounters that really transformed thousands of people's lives and even had the privilege to do one on site for a major corporate.
- I have taken quite a few young emerging leaders under my wing as mentees. There is nothing that excites me more than to see how some of them progressed exponentially in their careers and family lives.
- Public ministry in leadership development especially amongst men's groups and married couples. Liz and I are quite active on the latter in two groups i.e Partners 4 Life and Gushing Waters Fountain of Life where we serve on the advisory group.

- Sought after conference speaker where I address corporates and high impact meetings on current leadership challenges and how to respond within a context of a new values driven approach.
- Transformational training in corporates on issues of strategy, diversity, talent management and building winning teams.
- Writer of opinion articles on various media platforms and other publications with a strong emphasis on leadership development.

I can safely say that God has granted me the wisdom to have an absolute clear picture on how to move forward in my life after the Halftime experience. I know my core and capacity as well as the context in which it needs to be deployed. It gave me the credibility in becoming a trusted coach, mentor, and strategist in corporate, governmental and church circles. I came into my own and can certainly say I am enjoying the journey and my life took on greater significance. I hold fast to the wonderful promise of Ephesians 3: 20 (Passion Translation PT) *"Never doubt God's mighty power to work in you and accomplish all this. He will achieve infinitely more than your greatest request, your most unbelievable dream, and exceed your wildest imagination! He will outdo them all, for His miraculous power always energises you."*

Building meaning into your life is a matter of choice. Every moment in life is a teachable moment and we need to determine for ourselves how we are going to engage with that moment. If you have a sense of meaning:

- it frees you up from the success criteria of the world.
- you relate to people from a sense of vulnerability and inter-dependency.
- your relationship with your Creator is much more important than your ministerial output.
- you live out your true passion and your identity is not based on what others think you should be.
- you seize every opportunity to serve others above your own interests.

True meaning in life only comes through a living relationship with God. He does not only want you to operate in the realm of success but wants you to be somebody of significance. He wants you to live the life you were meant to live.

It won't happen by chance; you need to seek His face as I did, and He will help you to develop and pursue a compelling vision.

Chapter 6

THE POWER OF A NICHE

There is nothing that can distract from a leader's credibility than being inept and incompetent in executing the task at hand. Leaders need to have the capability and the necessary expertise to get things done properly. It is about operating in a spirit of excellence and becoming known in your specific field of expertise. The world is increasingly moving into high levels of specialisation, and you need to develop a niche position to enhance your credibility. You almost need to become the go-to person when a challenge surfaces on the radar because of your superior body of knowledge to give an appropriate solution. It will be important for you to continuously invest in the tools of your trade and hone your skills set at every available opportunity.

The story goes that once upon a time, a strong woodcutter asked for a job at a timber merchant. The pay was really good and so were the working conditions. This motivated the woodcutter to always give his best. His boss gave him an axe and a designated area to work in. The first day the woodcutter fell 18 trees. The boss was quite impressed and commended him for it. The next day the woodcutter came to work highly motivated but could not repeat the performance. He could only fell 15 trees. The third day was even worse because he could only do 11. The woodcutter thought that he might be losing his strength and approached his boss about the sudden downward slide in his performance. The boss asked him a simple question – when last did you sharpen your axe? The woodcutter was baffled by this question. But he admitted that he had no time to sharpen his axe because he was so busy concentrating on cutting as much trees as possible. Why am I telling you this story? To keep on top of your game, you need to periodically take out time to sharpen your axe through competency enhancement initiatives. These investments will ensure that you remain effective, relevant and produce credible outcomes. You need to look at every available opportunity to exchange notes with those that are leaders in your area of work for benchmarking purposes and identifying possible areas of new innovations that you can bring into the field. Busyness is not necessarily effectiveness.

I was thrown into the deep end of my leadership roles on many occasions. I could not blame apartheid and my previously disadvantaged background in perpetuity. I had to show up and equip myself with the requisite skills to deliver on expectations. At times I had to leave my family spending weeks at an overseas business school or attending a best practice conference so that I could remain current in my leadership approaches. There is also a level of self- empowerment where I am a keen reader and developed the habit to network with experts in a specific field where my knowledge of the subject is in a bit of a deficit. I made learning, a lifelong process and continuously set new targets on how to keep abreast on new trends that were emerging in the leadership landscape.

A disease called mediocrity

A few months ago, I found myself in the queue for close to two hours at a certain government department, to get a duplicate of an important document which I had lost. It was really an eye opener to a world which I am not frequently exposed to. I observed the approach of those behind the counters to their work, given the many people who come through their doors daily and are dependent on the vital service they deliver. This scenario triggered in my mind the whole question of excellence as opposed to the scenario of mediocrity that played itself out in front of me. Let me hasten to say, this phenomenon is not only confined to the public service but in all spheres of society where mediocrity is increasingly becoming contagious like a viral disease. I am sure that we all have at least a few experiences where service providers or institutions short-changed us on delivery.

At the heart of it all, is that we have been seduced by the status quo and have accepted second best as the norm. It gives us a false sense of comfort and familiarity. Being different is okay and you should not be anxious about possible consequences for challenging paradigms and pushing boundaries. To excel in life, warrants a qualitative change in mindset by declaring war on mediocrity. Mediocrity can subtly infiltrate your space and in the process your credibility can be compromised if left unchecked.

Being average is not an option, life is about continuous improvement in pursuit of excellence. You cannot go through life with an attitude that says "Well, I am not as bad as the others, at least I am still in the game." Most people do not live to their full potential because they are paralyzed by fear. These fears are subtle; the fear of failure, the fear of criticism or the fear of choosing excellence as a lifestyle to avoid offending people by doing the right thing. Paul wrote to his protégé Timothy about the best possible approach in this regard *"Do your best to present yourself to God as one approved, a worker who does not be ashamed and who correctly handles the word of truth"* 2 Timothy 2: 15(NIV). I believe what he may have wanted to say is Timothy my son, endeavour always to cultivate and improve your heart and mind. This will help to maintain your credibility and you will not become a reproach or embarrassment to Him from whom you purportedly received your mandate. You have been created for great glory, live it!

A society trapped in mediocrity is certainly in a downward spiral. It is also noticeably clear that it presents itself in such sophisticated ways because its sponsors have vested interests. There are certain people that can only thrive in an atmosphere of disorder. Once you bring order, stability and excellence to that environment, their limitations are exposed, and they become irrelevant. Some of the manifestations of mediocrity include:

- Defensiveness and always advancing numerous reasons why things should not be changed.
- Undermining authority and forever personalizing matters when called upon to account.

- High levels of deception and dishonesty. When confronted, the favourite default position is ABCD: Accuse, Blame, Condemn or Deny.
- Just doing enough to be on the safe side but not going out of your way to do anything exceptional that demonstrates innovation, urgency, and excellence.

The renowned Jim Collins states *"The signature of mediocrity is not an unwillingness to change; the signature of mediocrity is chronic inconsistency."* [29]

Let us dare to be different. When last have you done something for the first time in your life? There is a price to be paid to be different in an environment where mediocrity is entrenched. You will only be able to sacrifice when you have a compelling picture about serving a higher purpose. As a parent, you must model excellence to your children. If they see the example in you, it will inspire them and rid them from the attitude of laziness, entitlement, and mediocrity. Mediocrity feeds on a diet of self-interest and self-preservation. People and their wellbeing should always be at the centre of all your endeavours.

South Africa is a land with great potential. There are however quite a lot of unmet expectations and unfulfilled promises. One of the main contributing factors to this situation, is that we have allowed mediocrity to become mainstream in our public life. This is an ever-increasing phenomenon and sad to say, almost the new normal. We need to tackle the issue of mediocrity as a nation head-on, with the same vigour as that of tackling the outbreak of a pandemic disease. Mediocrity detracts from the credibility of our country to be regarded as a trailblazer in excellence on how we relate to each other and the outside world. It all starts with me and you individually sharpening our levels of competence and proficiency to carry it forward in our respective spheres of influence.

Excellence is a choice

"Excellence is never an accident. It is always the result of high intention, sincere effort, intelligent direction, skilful execution and the vision to see obstacles and opportunities" Dawkins Brown [30]

Fear can be the biggest impediment, in an environment in which you might appear as the odd one out when you choose to pursue excellence. Fear is a normal human emotion, and it can be healthy. It will trigger your adrenaline levels and stimulate you in a challenging environment. What is however unhealthy, is being in a perpetual state of fear. From a performance point of view, you cannot continually be preoccupied about other people's opinions and the possible consequences of challenging paradigms and pushing boundaries towards improved performance. These fears are very subtle; the fear of criticism, offence and potentially being labelled. Your destiny is determined by the quality of choices you make. Credible people choose excellence!

One of my favourite examples in the Bible on excellence other than Jesus, I found in the life of Daniel. He maintained an uncompromising lifestyle, serving in the courts of the king in a foreign land, yet he remained committed to his beliefs and principles. This earned him the respect of his superiors but also the wrath of some of his adversaries who plotted against him. He ended up in a den of lions for worshipping God and not a false idol, yet the Lord delivered him. In the final analysis his superior knowledge, exceptional performance and supernatural wisdom did not escape the attention of the king.

"Then this Daniel distinguished himself above the governors and satraps, because an excellent spirit was in him and the king gave thought to setting him over the whole realm" Daniel 6:3 (NKJV) God does not bless the mediocre, He blesses excellence. Excellence, motivated by love, honours God and inspires people. You have been created for great glory, start living it. For you to excel, you need to be ahead of the pack, see the bigger picture and continuously raise the bar higher.

Excellence first starts with you and me individually in our assignment in life. When we take it forward in our different spheres of influence with a sense of urgency and collective stewardship for our actions, we can make a difference in our village. A spirit of excellence greatly enhance your credibility and you can set new standards for continuous improvement.

"Whatever may be your task, work with at it heartily from the soul, as something done for the Lord and not for men. Knowing with all certainty that it is from the Lord and not from men that you will receive your real

reward. The One whom you are actually serving is the Lord. "(Colossians 3:23 -24 – Amplified AMP)

When somebody believes in you

The myth of the self-made man or woman has long been debunked in leadership circles. No person of significance in life, made it without the positive influence of others. Central in the whole scheme of things, is the key role of mentors.

My understanding about mentorship, is that these are real life exchanges that help those with lesser experience be guided by someone with more experience (not necessarily older) to discover their potential and pursue their purpose in life. In his book The Heart of Mentoring, David Stoddard gives a very succinct explanation as to why we need mentors.[31] He highlights three reasons that informs a mentoring relationship:

- To help me with my passion
- To help me with my pain
- To help me with my priorities.

I was indeed privileged that in the critical phases of my life, I had great mentors. These were men and women of a special kind who believed in me, took me under their wings and brought the best out of me. I want to pay tribute to two incredibly special men that I was privileged to have in my life. Firstly, Pastor Simpson Ngcizela who took me under his wings during the early days of my spiritual formation and in whose life, I saw the miraculous power of God being manifested in such a profound way. He literally took me as his son and we travelled widely together on Kingdom assignments. I recall one of my highlights being invited as a guest speaker through his recommendation, by the Tanzanian Kingdom Leadership Network in Dares Salaam to address a very prestigious conference in 2015. Then there was Professor Stef Coetzee who was a great fountain of wisdom during my early days in politics and later working with him in the leadership of the Afrikaanse Handels Instituut. They were God fearing men and both have passed on already. I will forever be indebted to them for the investment they have made in my life over many years.

It is important to note that investing in the younger generation is not just a good idea but is in fact a God- given mandate. One of the central tenets of the Great Commission is people development. It is this generation that is currently at the forefront of change in the world, determined to get ahead at an accelerated pace in life and constantly searching for the why part in any given situation. It is also a generation that is grappling with major socio-economic issues like racism, inequality, the environment, technology advancements to name but a few. They are therefore looking for role models worth emulating.

The Bible has many mentor related examples. One of my favourite examples is the one between Elijah and Elisha. The significance of this relationship was that Elisha had a huge hunger, passion, yearning and strong desire for the qualities of his mentor. He asked at Elijah's departure for a double portion of his anointing; that is, God's divine power, glory, confidence, boldness, and authority. I think one of the biggest tragedies in our current times, is that we are simply not hungry enough to emulate and mirror the values and divine attributes of our mentors. One almost gets a sense that people are just going through the motions, waiting for their chance to take over leadership.

Mentorship is not an event but a lifestyle whereby there is a deliberate and conscious engagement within the relationships that God placed us in. Allow me to share a few pointers in this regard:

1. Selecting a mentor must be a well-considered decision. You need to be sure that the individual has experience and maturity to guide you, demonstrate excellence in the area that you need assistance, has the time and energy to devote to you, believes in you and shares similar values with you.
2. There must be no ambiguity about role expectations. The ground rules must be agreed upon right up front and there must not be any misalignment of expectations.
3. Mentorship is a marathon not a 100-meter sprint. The journey is more important than the destination. Both parties need to have patience, perseverance, and persistence.

4. It is more of a heart journey than a head journey. A mentor understands that it is about sowing and impartation; hence motives are paramount. We do it for the right reasons and not as a fan club or merely looking for an audience dispensing expert advice.
5. Mentorship accords us an invaluable opportunity for mutual learning. I have often been astounded on how I had to abandon my own prejudices and unlearn things that I held on so dearly when exposed to the rationality and validity of a different point of view by someone I mentored. Nobody in life knows it all. Opening our own different worlds to each other, is such an enriching experience.
6. Both parties need to embrace the opportunity with a high degree of humility and never overestimate one's own importance. For the mentor, it is an affirmation of confidence and the mentee, an opportunity to unlock potential. It is powerful when somebody believes in us.

I would like to raise these two critical questions with you:
Who are you mentoring?
Who is mentoring you?

Are we having the right people on the bus?

In any area that you operate, it is imperative that you have an effective team working as a cohesive unit towards the accomplishment of a common goal. People with the requisite competencies and skills-set to enhance the credibility of your organisation. To frame it differently: Are we having the right people on the bus?

> *"Leaders of companies that go from good to great start not with where but with who. They start by getting the right people on the bus, the wrong people off the bus and the right people in the right seats."* Jim Collins [32]

On a frequent basis, tough questions are asked at a range of levels about the performance of sports teams (especially when you are a Liverpool or

Kaizer Chiefs fan), company boards and their executive teams, volunteers in non-profit organisations, educational institutions, political parties, church leadership and governments to name but a few. In leadership, it takes courage and discernment to facilitate a situation where we get the right people on the bus, get the wrong people off the bus, and ensure that the right people are in the right seats.

Not everyone can be on the bus and leaders must reconcile themselves with this reality. I am inherently a very relational person and thrives on doing things for and with people. Though undoubtedly one of my greatest strengths, it also occasionally became one of my greatest weaknesses. I can so easily develop a liking to someone and I tend to trust people too readily. I paid an extremely high premium for allowing people into my life based on a liking without doing sufficient due diligence to establish fit for purpose imperatives. There are very impressive individuals whom I later discovered to be bad team players. I encountered many a dominant personality who always assumes to be right and not accommodative of the constructive views of others. Then you have the egotistical type, who always bask in vain glory and totally discounts the contribution of other members of the team.

It has often taken quite a substantive amount of my time just to manage some of the above-mentioned contradictions. In many instances it not only distracted from the company's objectives but also put my own credibility at risk. To safeguard myself against some adverse eventualities, I adopted the following guidelines as to who will qualify for a boarding pass on my bus:

- Expectations should be spelt out up front so that there is no ambiguity about how we are going to relate to each other. Not everyone is necessarily the full package and I have learned not to harbour exaggerated expectations. I need to make a careful assessment what will be the opportunity cost to narrow any developmental gaps.
- We must share the same values, those uncompromisable and undebatable truths that direct our conduct. There will be instances where we might have strong differences of opinion on a specific matter but in the final analysis, our perspectives must always be calibrated against an agreed set of values.

- Having an objective and responsive mind-set facilitates innovative thinking in the group. There are those that are simply resistant to change. A perpetual sense of negativity can rub off on the rest of the team and it needs to be confronted quite early in the game.
- I do not like gatekeepers in an organisation that filter information before it reaches higher authority on the pretence that they have the ear of leadership. This perceived position of privilege creates parallel accountability structures and undermines the credibility of authority.
- Sharing the same vision with a high degree of loyalty to the cause, is one of the non-negotiables in my book. I want to have the assurance that when there is a breakdown or problem on the journey, some people will not expediently jump off the bus.

As we journey along, we should never take the passengers for granted. We live in an era where people can so easily drift from commitment. It is therefore of paramount importance to carefully consider at a personal level, who you give access to your life and at an organisational level, being rigorous about fit for purpose considerations. You are as good as the company you keep. One needs to appreciate that some talented and highly resourceful people that expressed an interest to journey with you and to whom you have issued a boarding pass, might not even turn up when the bus departs. That's alright. How many people have enthusiastically applauded you about your vision and pledged their support with a truckload of promises? But when it comes to implementation, they simply do not turn up. There might be key people in your life who started the journey with you but for some reason or the other, decide not to continue the journey with you. That is also fine. In any endeavour of note, no individual is bigger than the cause. Focus on those committed ones that are still on board by creating space and opportunity for them to reach their full potential. Never neglect an opportunity to affirm their contribution as you journey together in pursuit of greatness.

What are we saying to each other? Your credibility is greatly influenced by the quality of the team you assemble; people who are competent and able to subscribe to your quest for excellence. You must also make a special effort to remain current and on top of your game because today's excellence is tomorrow's mediocrity. Continually expand the horizons of your knowledge base. Read things you do not normally read about. The world is moving at such a rapid pace and there is such a massive explosion of knowledge. Hence learning should become a life- long process.

Credible leaders have the rare ability to spot potential and attach value to it. They are prepared to go the extra mile and invest time and resources through a dedicated process of mentoring. In the words of Marvin Ashton *"Be the one who nurtures and builds. Be the one who has an understanding and a forgiving heart and looks for the best in people. Leave people better than you found them."* [33]

PITSTOP

To enhance your leadership credibility, you must also create an environment where others can grow, be stretched, and continually be challenged. One of the defining moments of my leadership journey in this regard, was taught to me by the iconic Nelson Mandela. At a personal level, I had the privilege to interact with President Mandela on several occasions during my tenure as MEC of Finance and Economic Affairs in the North West Province. The one encounter that made the most profound impact on my life was on 28 March 1997, during President Mandela's state visit to the Prime Minister of India, Deve Gowda. I was coincidentally also in India at that time, being hosted by our then High Commissioner to India Jerry Matjila, for a study trip on Small Medium and Micro Enterprise (SMME) development. Madiba on hearing that I am also in India, requested that I be part of his official delegation to meet the Indian Prime Minister.

This was arguably one of the highlights of my political career. I was really taken aback by this gesture. I made sure I got up early that morning, shaved myself twice and even ironed my own shirt to ensure it was in tip top shape. Though overwhelmed by the occasion and being on my best behaviour, when I entered the room Madiba made me feel so welcome as he enquired about my trip and how things were in our province. As the discussions ultimately ensued, I just marvelled to see the man at work as he engaged his counterpart from India. I soaked in every bit of his logical reasoning and wise counsel given to a colleague without being prescriptive. His deep insight about geo-political dynamics, was just a marvel to listen to.

Madiba was under no obligation to invite me to be part of his delegation, but he regarded me as sufficiently important to be part of his team. It says a lot about the measure of the man. Many of us shut the door on others when we are at the pinnacle of our leadership role and everything just revolves around me, myself, and I.

I learned the following critical lessons out of that encounter with Madiba which from then onwards, greatly informed my leadership approach:

1. Leaders need to appreciate the potential in others and create space and opportunity for them to grow. Tony Dungy puts it so aptly *"Mentor leaders look beyond themselves, focusing on the people they lead and where they should be going together."* [34]
2. Leaders need to create an atmosphere that is encouraging and affirming. What struck me, his delegation consisted of only five of us and during the introduction, he specifically introduced me as one of his provincial ministers of finance. I was not just anybody, I was one of his. There are leaders that just tolerate you but never affirm you.
3. The greatest impartation of a leader is not in what he or she says but how he or she acts. Each one of us has an obligation in our leadership journey, to identify people whose conduct and example is worth emulating. Paying close attention on how they respond to different sets of circumstances, can give us valuable insights for our own leadership development. You cannot surround yourself with mediocrity and expect excellence in your leadership output. You will only be as good as the people you spend time with.
4. Great leaders have a generational perspective in mind. I was just about three years into political office and yet Madiba saw me

as sufficiently important to expose me to this valuable teaching moment. He was mindful about equipping others to keep the momentum of what he stood for, beyond his lifespan. In the words of Dr Myles Munroe "*The greatest act of leadership is mentoring. No matter how much you may learn, achieve, accumulate or accomplish, if it dies with you, then you are a generational failure.*"[35]

Chapter 7

DARING COURAGEOUSLY

In my leadership journey, I have seen a lot of movers and shakers who hop from one company to the other. On closer observation, it is quite interesting to note that their so-called successes were only registered in a cycle of moonshine and roses. They usually jump ship when there is the slightest hint of a headwind and conveniently migrate to safer options.

One's credibility is greatly enhanced if you can navigate through a downward cycle back into high levels of profitability or performance. It is out of these hard knocks and difficult learning experiences that you will not only gain the respect of those you lead but you will also establish credibility with external stakeholders. We have seen how many businesses took tremendous strain during the Covid-19 pandemic. Some had to take tough decisions to restructure their business environment and rationalise some of their activities to stay afloat. Other institutions like education, churches, families, sports, and entertainment…were all put under tremendous strain and had to innovate to stay in the game. It is in these sets of circumstances that the true character of leaders is tested. This requires high levels of courage and perseverance.

Courage speaks of a spirit of determination and persistence; it is the ability to persevere under difficult circumstances and not give up that easily. It speaks of bravery and to have valour; to be fearless, daring, and bold. Leaders with a courageous spirit have the will of mind to make the hard decisions dictated by the times. Even at a personal level, you and I will face difficult circumstances and if we want to maintain our credibility, courage needs to become a way of life. Temporary setbacks are not fatal, it only expands your reservoir of learning experiences. Informed by those experiences, you will be much better equipped given a similar set of circumstances.

Our world is beset with a host of what appears to be insurmountable challenges. It will require from you and me to be fearless, daring, and bold; to stand our ground where compromise is such a convenient option. Life has its highs and lows. Never give up and lose perspective when navigating through tough and challenging situations. Keep standing... notwithstanding. Life is inherently a risky business. The word risk implies uncertainty and life does not always prepare you and me adequately for uncertainty. You might have travelled to work this morning and might not return home due to a fatal accident. Your marriage might be smooth sailing and suddenly either you or your spouse is hit by a dreaded disease... this is the business called life.

It is time to show up!

I ordinarily like to be busy and have my hands in numerous endeavours at any given point in time. Being a maintenance guy is not my scene and I thrive on starting organisations from scratch, getting it to optimal functionality and handing over when things are on an upward trend. The journey has not always been smooth sailing and on many occasions, I had to make tough choices during very turbulent times. I have long ago come to the realisation that in leadership there are certain responsibilities that you simply cannot delegate or outsource. You must show up and do the things others are unwilling to do. You must be capable of leading people to places that they never thought they would go.

One of the barriers that prevents leaders from reaching their maximum potential, is a phenomenon called risk aversion. This occurs when fear of loss stifles our attempts to gain. Fear can rob us of many life changing opportunities because we lead conservatively and try to play it safe. Our brain is normally wired that way. From my personal experience, I can without any fear of contradiction state that I tend to remember bad things more easily than good. Regrettably, we bring this type of orientation into our decision processes as well and our decisions are framed to prevent loss instead of achieving gain.

To be effective in your leadership role, there is a price to be paid. Larry Osborne once made a profound statement *"The most striking thing about highly effective leaders is how little they have in common. What one swears by another warns against. But one trait stands out: effective leaders are willing to take risks."*[36] Maintaining the status quo and playing it safe is simply not good enough to inspire those you are leading, to conquer new ground and maximise their potential.

I will be the first to admit that overcoming risk aversion is sometimes easier said than done. There are always those lingering questions about – What if? Why fix a thing that is not broken? We are still in the pack, why upset the applecart?

Effective leadership is about continuous improvement and shifting the boundaries. A safety net builds the confidence of trapeze artists. It does not prevent them from falling, but it prevents the fall from being fatal. They can in their preparation, try out things that they had never done before and stretch themselves to the maximum. No wonder when it comes showtime, we all marvel at some of the most daring acts on display by these artists. If you know that failure is not fatal, you will know that it is safe to take risks. Risks that will not only take away the breath of your audience but also inspire you to greater heights. The following aspects greatly assisted me on my leadership journey to construct appropriate safety nets:

1. Make risk taking a lifestyle: Destiny is determined by being consistently faithful in the small and routine things in life. Those tasks that are unnoticed and appear to be insignificant, prepare you to be battle ready for bigger challenges in life. In 1 Samuel 17 we read the account of how David slayed the giant Goliath. Talk about risk taking, this was indeed a serious one. In presenting his resume to King Saul, David gave an account of how he killed a lion and, on another occasion even a bear when the sheep were

under attack which his father left under his care. Far away from the spotlight, he was in training which gave him the confidence to ultimately win one of the most ambitious duels in history.

2. Be prepared to win the battle within you: One of the biggest challenge leaders face daily, is the battle in our minds. It is almost a proverbial war game where our energy is directed towards defence, survival, escape and whatever coping mechanism possible. You need to engage daily in those disciplines that will nourish and strengthen your mentality.
3. Be intentional with what you fill your mind with: If you think that you are going to lose, you have already lost before the game even started. Philippians 4: 8 (MSG) *"Summing it all up friend, I'd say you'll do best by filling your minds on things true, noble, reputable, authentic, compelling, gracious – the best not the worst; the beautiful not the ugly; things to praise not to curse."*
4. Thrive through teamwork: You are not the full package. Allow your weaknesses to be augmented by the strengths of others. Working with a great team de-risked my endeavours.
5. Failure fosters growth: Some of my greatest learning experiences come from the situations where things went completely wrong. I thought that I had everything under control and all bases covered, only to discover that I overlooked something that caused me to fail. Failure is not fatal but provides us with invaluable opportunities for growth. People who are afraid to fail, always play it safe and rob themselves and others of opportunities for growth and development.

Are you willing to put yourself on the line if need be? Are you ready for the possible criticisms, rejection, sweat, toil, and tears to do things others are not prepared to do? Start writing that book you always wanted to write, compose that song, mentor that young person who everybody is saying is rebellious, start that business, go on that adventurous trip, sever ties with that destructive friendship, start with that community development project. Ask me, there is nothing as exhilarating than to know that you mustered up the courage, stepped out of your comfort zone, conquered your deepest fears, and made an impact on the lives of others.

Cowardice detracts from one's credibility. Show me your scars and your T- shirt and then I will be able to make a more balanced assessment of your level of credibility. Let the real you show up!

There is meaning in the mess

I do not know about you, but quite a few times in my life I had to ask myself "How did I really get into this mess?" There are situations in life that are so overwhelming, inconvenient and slows us down on this journey of life. Life can be a messy business for example the unexpected death of a loved one, your teenage daughter becoming pregnant in her matric year, sudden retrenchment from your job, your spouse becoming addicted to gambling or pornography, being diagnosed with a dreaded disease, the enterprise you worked so hard to build over so many years unexpectedly being placed under business rescue etc. Am I talking to the right audience?

The other day I listened to an illustration by Os Hillman that drives this point home so aptly. He stated that when a major road construction project takes place in a crowded city street, it appears to be absolutely chaos. It is inconvenient, slow moving and tends to get us irritated because it appears that we are moving much slower than we like. It is ugly and so much of what we see is torn up. But when we look at the same area a few months or years later, we see why the construction was necessary. It makes life so much better for those who would use the road. We will not always understand why we find ourselves in certain messy situations and its impact on our journey moving forward. You are not defined by your current reality; there is a bigger picture that is about to unfold in your life. Yours is to embrace the process with persistence and determination.

There is no doubt in my mind that adversity builds character, but this is dependent on your response to the circumstances at hand. One of the men who has inspired me greatly is Abraham Lincoln. In 1831 he lost his job; in 1832 he was defeated in a run for Illinois State Legislature. His business was liquidated in 1833; his wife died in 1835 and he suffered a nervous breakdown in 1836. He was defeated in a run for Illinois Speaker in 1838; defeated in a run for the United States Congress in 1843; defeated in a run for the United States Senate in 1854; defeated in a run for the

Vice-President of the United States in 1856. In 1860 Abraham Lincoln was elected as the President of the United States of America. What a remarkable journey of courage, tenacity, and endurance. His legacy as President of the most influential nation on the planet, is still honoured. He was not defined by his failures and setbacks, but relentlessly pursued his dream. Adversity certainly builds character. As a believer, one needs to appreciate that sometimes God will allow these challenges and obstacles on our journey of life to build our character. God is more interested in what we become than our comfort.

When you find yourself in a messy situation, maintain the momentum. Even when you are uncertain of the outcome, move forward with boldness. Do not get stuck in the traffic just because you are irritated by the inconvenience of the road construction. During these times, you might have to implement drastic changes. No matter how uncomfortable or unpopular the changes might be, be courageous enough to take it on.

Some of the messy situations in life can also bring about a paradigm shift in our lives. Bill Donahue describes it as the ABC of Deep Personal Change:

- Admit that you are powerless against the current onslaught.
- Believe that a Power greater than yourself can deliver and restore you.
- Conform your will to God's by turning your life and will over to Him. [37]

Do not stop dreaming. God has given you creative ability, therefore see beyond your current reality. God does not give us all the answers immediately and does not necessarily jump to our timeline. Patience is the key to navigating through the messy moments.

There is meaning in the mess. It is for this reason that Paul whose life was characterised by many setbacks could boldly proclaim in Romans 8: 28 (NIV) *"And we know that in all things, God works for the good of those who love Him who have been called according to His purpose."*

NB. All things. I witnessed on countless occasions in my own life how God turned my mess into a message. Informed by all these life experiences,

I can now engage more authentically with those finding themselves in a rough patch. It is really humbling to realise that whatever I have overcome and accomplished, is only by His grace.

Persistence – the game changer

One of the most intriguing realities in life, is that one cannot predict how someone will finish the race from how he or she began with absolute certainty. Certain people have been born with the proverbial golden spoon in their mouths, yet their lives turn out to be a monumental failure notwithstanding all the advantages. Conversely, others might come from an environment of deprivation and lack, yet their lives turn out to be a legendary success. Does this sound familiar?

Persistence is that rare quality that allows someone to continue doing something even though it is difficult or opposed by other people. Billions of people around the world are today enjoying the convenience of the electric light bulb. It was born out of the unrelenting persistence of Thomas Edison, who after more than a thousand attempts, took the failures as learning opportunities until he produced the perfect light bulb in 1878.

Ralph Waldo Emmerson once said: "*That which we persist in doing becomes easy to do; not that the nature of the thing has changed, but that our power to do it has increased.*" [38] Strength comes from struggle, be it physical, emotional, spiritual, financial etc. If we are not regularly subjected to challenges, like a muscle that is not frequently exercised, our capacity will progressively waste away.

Teams that normally win tough games and have a pedigree of success have high impact players in their ranks. Likewise, in the game called life, we also need to have impact to win the ultimate prize. The following are some of the characteristics of high impact players:

1. Quitting is not an option to them.

When a player is selected to represent his country, he must put life and limb on the line. Likewise, as someone representing the Kingdom, God promised that He will never leave you or forsake you, regardless of the obstacles. You are more than a conqueror because the Greater One resides in you.

One of the most inspiring stories I read in 2020 to orientate my mind on the upcoming Olympics, is about John Akhwari. In 1968 he represented Tanzania in the Olympics Marathon race in Mexico. At the 30 km mark as the race accelerated and athletes jostled to the front, he was pushed and fell badly, injuring his knee and suffered a dislocation. He however hobbled along up to the finish line. The people in the streets of Mexico could not believe their eyes what they were seeing and continued to cheer him on. Though he came last of the 17 athletes that finished the race, it is significant to note that 79 athletes actually started the race. When he ran into the stadium almost an hour after the winner crossed the line, there were only a few thousand people left but he was welcomed with a thunderous applause right up to the finishing line. When interviewed by a television presenter after his race as to why he continued running with a dislocated knee and enduring excruciating pain, he responded "*My country did not send me 5000 miles to start the race; they sent me 5000 miles to finish the race.*" This story became legendary, epitomising the spirit of the Olympics and put his name firmly in the annals of sporting history. Quitting was not an option for John Akhwari and he can confidently be regarded as being "more than a conqueror."

2. Commitment to the game plan

Solomon was known to be a mover and a shaker in his days. How come that the book of Ecclesiastes, reflects so much disillusionment and discontent in his life? In 1 Kings 11 we read about his demise and death where it is recorded that he had 700 wives and 300 concubines who turned his heart to other foreign gods, in total violation of God's commandments. Impact players finish strong because they stick to the instructions and game plan of the coach. In Solomon's case, it was quite evident that he did not stick to the "Coach's" instructions hence he did not experience any sense of fulfilment during the latter part of his life. If we want to make an impact and finish strong in our assignment in life, we need to remain committed to the prescripts of the Word of the Lord.

3. Power of proclamation

If you say you are a loser, you have already lost before the game has even started. *"Death and life are in the power of the tongue and those who love it, will eat its fruit. "* Proverbs 18:21 (NKJV). People of impact establish in their hearts that they can be victorious and then speak to it continuously over themselves and act accordingly.

Discovering your destiny is not an academic exercise but a matter of intense (and intentional) life engagement. You therefore need to be clear why you have been selected for the squad. It will require of you to demonstrate high levels of persistence and become a player of impact. It is that relentless pursuit of your destiny regardless of the obstacles that defines you. Winning is a choice and so is losing. It is not over until God says it is over.

Turning tragedy into triumph

Life will at times throw us a curved ball that totally disrupt our plans and take the wind out of our sails. If we are not careful, it will hurt us for the rest of our lives and keep us in captivity to never regain what we have lost. When you lost your job after having such a fulfilling tenure for many years, you might think that there is no way in which you will get such an opportunity again. A bitter divorce might evoke the question as to whether you will be able to trust someone again. Losing all you had on what was once a lucrative business, might cause you to give up and prevent you from trying something new again. A nasty racist inspired incident against you might cause you to throw in the towel and not reach out to people transculturally and fall into the trap of generalisations by saying - all of them are like that.

I read an article a couple of years ago and the essence of it stayed with me all these years. The founder of Facebook and one of the world's most iconic business figures Mark Zuckerberg, became a father for the first time in 2015. During the pregnancy of his wife Priscilla, he took a moment to share on his Facebook page about their struggle over the preceding years to have a baby. His wife suffered multiple miscarriages. Mark described the heart-breaking loss as follows *"You feel so hopeful when you learn you're going to have a child. You start imagining who they'll become and dreaming of hopes of their future. You start making plans and then they are gone.*" [39]

Well, on 1 December 2015 his wife gave birth to a healthy baby daughter called Max. On the same day of his daughter's birth, he wrote a 2200-word letter to his Max starting with the following sentence *"Dear Max, your mother and I don't have the words to describe the hope you give us for the future. Your new life is full of promise and we hope you will be happy and healthy so you can explore it fully.*" In celebration of his daughter's birth, he vowed to give away 99% of his shares in Facebook during his life for "*Advancing human potential and promoting equality.*" His current net worth as at end January 2021 was $95,6 billion. What an awesome turnaround in overcoming what appeared to be an insurmountable struggle.[40]

It is alright to ask the question "Why?" There is nothing wrong to determine where your heart is and try to get to grips with what went wrong. It is therefore not forbidden to ask these tough questions. Though suffering is simply not a good thing, God can use it to accomplish good out of it far above what you might have imagined. Strength grows in the moments when we think we simply cannot go on but keep going anyway. No one is exempted from trials, tests, and tribulations. It can happen to the best of us; ask Mark Zuckerberg. I can write volumes of navigating through my own share of serious challenges in my life. There is a testimony in your test and a message in your mess. Embrace reality with hope.

You have come too far to give up now

Discouragement is the opposite of courage and I do not want to discount its reality and impact. It sometimes hits you when least expected but at times it can also build-up gradually occasioned by inner turmoil. Maybe today you are considering submitting your resignation letter because of constant setbacks in your work relationships and aspirations. Given some of the vexing socio-economic challenges in our country, you cannot wait for the Covid-19 pandemic to be over because you are contemplating emigration. Unmet expectations in your marriage and perceived incompatibility might have triggered the thought of a divorce. You want an exit strategy because of all the hurt, disappointments and betrayal and just don't have the energy left to give it one more try. These can be quite debilitating matters.

Just as in nature, life is about cycles and seasons. Even in the depth of disillusionment and discouragement, one needs to know that it is but for a season. Our attitude towards a specific season in life will determine how successfully we navigate it. Some of us will remember that just prior to South Africa's first democratic elections in 1994, some people from certain sectors of society stock-piled canned foods, water, gas stoves and all manner of stuff out of fear what might happen when a new Black led government will come into power. We have since had five successful elections after the first one. Their worst fears did not materialize, and life went on in our beloved country. By this I do not mean that we don't have challenges at this point in our country, but the dooms day prophecies never saw the light of day.

Coming from a seriously disadvantaged background with all its constraints, I would never have imagined the things I have accomplished by God's grace. I was written off on quite a few occasions, my family life has at times been under severe threat and strain, my faith has been stretched; yet I am still standing. Never forget the journey you have already traversed and draw inspiration from the rich tapestry of learning experiences.

The mighty King David was once faced with fierce opposition and threats when the Amalekites destroyed parts of the land. In 1Samuel 30: 6 (KJV) we read "*...But David encouraged himself in the Lord.*" I do not have any doubts about how David was able to respond in such a courageous manner amid these circumstances. The greater part of the book of Psalms is a living record of how he always encouraged himself in the Lord when persecuted, rejected, attacked, and betrayed. Encouragement is the most powerful antidote for discouragement and disillusionment. I would strongly recommend that when you wake up in the morning, reflect on at least one good thing or even more that happened in your life over the last 24 hours and encourage yourself in it. The mere fact that you are still alive right now amidst the onslaught of arguable the most devastating pandemic over the last few decades, is something to be thankful about.

Quitting is not an option. Each one of us has been given a specific assignment in life. Quitting on unfinished business can lead to a life of endless regret and being a prisoner of "if only". Never make a major decision in a season of turmoil. Wait for the dust to settle. Your objectivity can be clouded by taking a decision out of compulsion and you will not be able to see the wood for the trees. If possible, take some time out to gain a fresh perspective. It is also helpful to seek wise counsel from someone you trust and whose opinion you value.

Recognise that there are many people who do care. You are not defined by the adverse experience with one or a few individuals. I draw inspiration daily from the kind gestures, compliments, affirmation, respect and appreciation from family, friends and sometimes from people least expected. It is for their sake that I am not prepared to throw in the towel and keep pressing on in pursuit of my mission in life. There is just too much at stake. Do not quit on your career, marriage, family, life assignment, business, close friends, community, health, country, faith... Your breakthrough might just be a few moments away. You have come too far to give up now. Romans 12: 12 (NIV) *"Be joyful in hope, patient in affliction, faithful in prayer."*

Leadership is about influence. It is that rare ability to equip people to do what they thought was impossible. The major responsibility of leadership is to do the correct things which others are unwilling to do; the proverbial putting yourself on the line. It is called crunch time. I trust that through God's grace and divine wisdom, you will be able to make the right call in your sphere of influence. I trust that you will boldly and with a spirit of daring courageously, engage with the short-term pain in pursuit of the long-term gain.

PITSTOP

There was a massive strike of general workers at Tshepong Hospital organised in 1992 and hundreds of general workers lost their jobs under the old labour laws of the previous regime. They sat for almost seven months in the wind and cold outside the gates of Tshepong Hospital. It was not a pleasant sight to see some of the old ladies that I grew up with for more than fifteen years experiencing this kind of hardship. Some of them were due for pension in a year's time.

I still have a vivid picture in my mind about a specific day during the initial phases of the strike, when the workers staged sit-ins for a few days in certain strategic places of the hospital. These are normal union tactics and did not have much of an effect on our work routine. By then I oversaw the Casualty and Outpatient Departments. I just saw a commotion in the corridors as riot police unleashed dogs on general staff members and began hitting them. In the background I heard teargas canisters going off and there was chaos throughout. The hospital resembled a war zone. I got reports from my colleagues how dogs were unleashed right in the wards as they were pursuing the striking workers. Some of the workers escaped because the nurses dressed them up in theatre attire and put them in empty beds as if they were just coming back from theatre. What broke my heart that day, was when I was standing on the other side of a big glass window and saw how a tall and well-built White policeman gave one of my student nurses a vicious slap as she staggered to find her feet again. He continued to scream profanities at her whilst she was crying profusely. That picture of me standing there helpless and not being able to say anything or do anything to help one of my students who just happened to be near the cafeteria at that time, left me scarred for quite a long time.

Those of us on the inside mobilised as much as possible for the worker's reinstatement until the labour union succeeded in getting an arbitration hearing. Judge Cathy Satchwell was appointed as arbitrator and evidence was presented over five days. I was called by the evidence leader of the union Fikile Majola on a Wednesday night. We met secretly at the nurse's residence with what had become the informal internal leadership core from the nurse's side. He gave us a comprehensive briefing about the case and wanted to clarify certain things with us about the sequence of events. He told us how bad their case looked at that point in time because the predominantly White senior management had given some scathing evidence against the workers. He challenged us that if Black managers did not stand up, the workers were sunk. I was already in management by then and consented to testify on behalf of the workers. One of my colleagues the late Phillip Phoyane, a very courageous man, and a colleague that I was fond of since student days, also raised his hand to join me as a witness.

What informed my consent in this regard had nothing to do with showing off or wanting to be somebody. It was my humble contribution in pursuit of justice because the worker's demands were legitimate and reasonable against the suppressive labour laws of the apartheid regime. It was also to be a truthful voice on what transpired. The key witnesses in the State's case from management's side were not even on site and ran the hospital remotely by two-way radios. When I was called in to testify, I gave a truthful account of what I saw on that day, including the incident of police brutality on innocent patients and not forgetting the heart wrenching incident of my student. I rebutted all the major allegations because the key managers at the peak of the strike ran away, and we were left alone while the police were running amok with dogs and high levels of intimidation right inside the wards. God really gave Phillip and I great wisdom and courage that day. I will never forget how some of the old ladies came to me after my testimony at the hearing with tears in their eyes, hugging and thanking me for standing up for truth and justice. The arbitrator ruled in favour of the workers, and they were all reinstated. Courage has a price tag. From then onwards, I was never considered for promotion anymore notwithstanding my on-going superior performance.

It was such a great and heart - warming experience for me to visit Tshepong Hospital just a few months after my appointment as the first MEC of Finance in the North West Province with Premier Molefe and the MEC of Health – the late Dr. Molefi Sefularo. As I passed the very same office that day at the nurse's residence where we met in very desperate times with Fikile, I could not help but think of how God rewarded me for my courage not only on this incident but a host of others when working at Tshepong. I could address my former colleagues with a high degree of credibility and our delegation worked with them through some challenges which were still latent effects of our history. Today Tshepong is still the apex tertiary hospital in the North West Province and I look back on 17 years of making a small contribution under very difficult and trying circumstances. As for Fikile Majola, today he is the Deputy Minister of Trade and Industry in our country. We normally reminisce when we bump into each other about those days that our courage and tenacity had not failed us when the material conditions of our time demanded it from us.

Chapter 8

GRACEFUL COMMUNICATION

Our credibility is profoundly shaped by the way we communicate. To maintain your credibility, you must be able to articulate your intentions with such precision and power in a compelling, persuasive yet graceful manner. Effective communication is done with care, concern, and sensitivity.

Communication is as vital to your credibility as your heart is to your body. An adult heart pumps on average 6000 – 7500 litres of blood daily through the body. This brings about two major effects. The arterial system carries not only oxygen-rich blood but all the vital nutriments to sustain the body. Whereas the venous system removes all the carbon dioxide and any other harmful waste products from the cells into the various organs to get rid of it. Likewise, in effective communication we do not just bring encouragement, motivation, understanding and ignite passion in people's lives. Sometimes communication also carries with it an element of rebuke, correction, discipline, and accountability to remove those things that can be harmful to our future well-being. Imagine if your heart stopped to pump, it can be fatal. Similarly, if we stop communicating effectively, our leadership becomes redundant, and our credibility vanishes.

Do not be a coward – confront!

The worse advice I ever received in life, is to avoid confrontation at all costs. I am naturally a nice and likeable person. I was never a bully at school and people were always generally well disposed to my wit and wicked sense of humour. The word confrontation in my book, denoted hostility, ferocious arguments, and some sort of low- key civil war; a situation best left alone. I remember in my primary school days when it was customary for boys who were aggrieved about some silly argument, to settle it at an undisclosed venue after school, by slugging it out like ancient pugilists. I was always one of the most enthusiastic spectators but made sure to never be involved in a bare- knuckled contest.

I don't know about you but confronting people head-on is not always the easiest thing to do because it may become a bit messy, and we do not have any guarantees what the outcome might be. I do not like unnecessary drama and the last thing on my mind, is to live my life as one of the leading actors in a horror movie. I prefer leaving such vexatious things to sort themselves out with minimum involvement from my side.

Regrettably in real life, certain things cannot just be left to chance in the hope that they will sort themselves out. I am convinced that there is an obligation on any responsible person to face up and deal with a recurring problem or difficult situation that might pose a risk moving forward. Even Jesus did not shy away from confrontation. He dealt decisively with the money changers and dove sellers because of His disgust at what they had made of God's house of prayer.

Your credibility will be increasingly eroded if you shy away from dealing with the difficult questions and hope they will just disappear. *"You will find peace not by trying to escape your problems, but by confronting them courageously. You will find peace not in denial, but in victory."*[41] Donald Walters

Difficult conversations can cause anxiety because it is not always comfortable. At times the risks may be high, and we are not guaranteed of what the outcome might be.

I am sure at some stage of your leadership journey you also had to or will in the future deal with some exceedingly difficult conversations. Wherever there is a high expectation environment, difficult conversations are inevitable. In relationships there is a constant need to have these difficult conversations; we avoid it at our peril. It is not a matter of me versus you but a matter of us versus a problem that might erode the cohesiveness of the relationship. The wise King Solomon wrote many years ago in Proverbs 27:17 (NIV) *"As iron sharpens iron, so one person sharpens another."*

The benefit of rubbing two iron blades together is that the edges become sharper and more efficient in its intended purpose. We sometimes need intense engagement with others to help us regain focus and clarity of thought, ignite our passion, protect us from potential harm, navigate best possible options, energize us to take on new challenges and assurance of support on our journey. Sharpening ourselves through engagement with others, should be done sensibly and with sensitivity. In the final analysis, it is the courage of our conviction to initiate corrective action timeously, that will greatly assist us in remaining on the cutting edge of our purpose.

Confrontation can be healthy. Confrontation can enhance trust if a group knows that no one is beyond reproach and that there is space and opportunity to honestly ventilate matters that can potentially erode the group's cohesiveness. Please be mindful of the following to elicit a constructive outcome:

1. It is about the issue and not the person. As in sporting terms – play the ball and not the man.
2. What are my motives?
   Is it to win a debate or engage in real and meaningful dialogue? Is my engagement punitive or restorative? Do I just want to perform in front of an audience or really solicit an honest opinion?
3. Prepare adequately.
   - Write down the main points. Avoid assumptions or generalizations; points should be factual and concise. Ascertain your own understanding and attitude about the situation or the individual involved. How would I have liked to be treated if I was on the other side of the equation?
   - Appropriate setting.
   - Arrange for a place where you can have an unhindered engagement with sufficient time at your disposal. Email

correspondence should never be a substitute for real engagement. Once confirmed, act and do not postpone indiscriminately.

- Prayer

Ask for God's wisdom, guidance, and responsive hearts.

4. The quicker you deal with a matter, the better the chance of a speedy resolution. The issues should be dealt with timeously and do not wait until it grows a beard.
5. Do not cloud the issue; deal with one matter at a time and stick to the facts. Long preambles dilute the impact of your engagement.
6. Keep your emotions in check and communicate with care and concern.
7. Always give the other party a fair opportunity to give their side of the story. Nothing can be gained if you go into an engagement with fixed and preconceived notions.
8. Once you agree on a course of action, validate it, and give continuous feedback on progress registered. If there are still gaps in your progress, work on alternative options.

Not all confrontations might end positively. However, we cannot cowardly shy away from confronting the real issues of life. We need to speak the truth in love when confronting complex and difficult issues.

The success or failure in any relationship is dependent on how genuine and sincere we can engage in meaningful conversations, even the most difficult ones. If we do not walk in relational integrity by having to sometimes ask the hard questions when challenges come our way - blaming, naming, and shaming will be our default position. Let us not shy away from speaking the truth in love. Keep your motives pure, your content truthful, your tone neutral and have a gracious attitude.

Let the discussions begin!

You cannot lead if you cannot listen

It is somehow assumed that when you are in a leadership position, you are expected to solve people's problems and always have all the answers on your fingertips. This has instinctively led to a situation where most leaders have developed the habit of talking first and in most cases provide a cut and paste response without having a firm grasp of what the real issues are all about. Though there is a legitimate expectation on leaders to respond to issues promptly and appropriately, you cannot solve a problem well without listening well. Credible leaders are those who have learned the art of listening with a purpose. Mike Myatt puts it so aptly *"Want to become a better leader? Stop talking and start listening. Being a leader should not be viewed as a licence to increase the volume or rhetoric. Rather astute leaders know there are far more gained by surrendering the floor than by dominating it."*[42]

My understanding of the word "listening" is about lending an ear and making a concerted effort to attentively hear something. I will be the first to admit that it is not always that easy. Our senses are continuously assailed by so many distractions and listening has become an unfortunate casualty in our day and age. Effective and active listening is a conscious and deliberate act that requires us to be alert and alive to the environment in which we find ourselves. One of the most underutilized tools in the armoury of a leader, is the art of listening. There is nothing that can enhance your influence and credibility more than people feeling that you care and take the time to comprehensively listen to them, without any preconceived notions.

We can deprive ourselves of valuable learning experiences if we engage in selective listening; only listening to those things that tickle our own fancy. By engaging in reflective listening, we create space and opportunity to evaluate various points of view that will inform an appropriate course of action. It can also challenge our own paradigms, helping us to unlearn outdated practices and expose us to new and fresh approaches towards the resolution of a problem. The upside of effective listening is that it engenders relational integrity where it is not a train smash if my views as a leader are challenged. In such a relationship of trust, I will not hesitate to acknowledge when others have more superior insights than mine on a specific issue and gladly tap into the collective wisdom of my group for the common good.

When we take the time to hear people out, we value them by showing them love and respect. As we truly listen to them, we can learn why they believe what they do. This helps us to get a glimpse into their lives. As we are listening, it is unwise and shows immaturity to come up with a rebuttal while they are talking. It is important to truly listen and think about what you hear the person saying. Drafting our response while they are still talking is like preparing to debate them. The ultimate objective we want to achieve in attentive listening, is that the two people coming together value each other more than they care about being right.

Learning someone's reasons will help us to see their point of view and prevents us from veering into premature judgements. If someone shares their "why" behind their beliefs in something you do not necessarily subscribe to, consider the background they're sharing. People often land on their worldviews and specific stances because of their upbringing, which include both positive and negative experiences. When we allow ourselves to step into their world, even if it is just for a few minutes, we are less likely to be annoyed and pass judgement. Empathy is a key component to a healthy relationship. It is the capacity to imagine the feelings someone else had, though you haven't actually felt them yourself. Expressing it allows us to understand a different point of view, and to ultimately represent Jesus well to those who do not know Him.

If we master the art of effective listening, it will also enhance our sense of discernment. Words form a small part of the communication value chain. There are critical non-verbal cues that we should discern meticulously which carry at times, greater meaning than the spoken word. Pay special attention to body language, tone of voice, eye contact and any other underlying emotions. When we listen with intent, we do not only connect at a superficial level but at the heart level. It is quite interesting to note that the very letters that spells the word silent is used to spell listen. Just think about it.

The highest form of listening is self-reflection. If you want to make progress in your life, you must develop the habit of learning to be quiet, settle down and turn off all possible distractions and listen to what your soul says to you. As I journeyed through life, I came to the realization that the following areas need continuous self – reflection:

- Thoughts: Everything starts with a thought. It is therefore important to reflect on those things that will nurture your thought processes. What are you reading? What TV programmes are you watching? Which people are you constantly in conversation with? What activities do you engage in to stimulate you mentally?

- Emotions: All of us have an off day at times. If there are however perpetual mood swings prevalent in our lives, we need to give it some attention and get to the root of the problem. Things like anxiety, fear, insecurity, and guilt might be symptomatic of a deep-seated problem.
- My body: Some people think that working 18 hours a day continuously is a virtue. We need to maintain a balance and give attention to any signals of undue physical and mental fatigue, lack of concentration, anorexia, insomnia to name but a few. Early detection can avert a lot of adverse complications.
- Passion barometer: Passion is the fuel of life and gives us the urge to relentlessly pursue our dreams. When you lose your passion, life can come to a standstill. Sometimes it might just be that you have overstayed your brief in a specific assignment and fell into maintenance mode. The most honest thing to do is to move on and reinvent yourself.

People engage in a multiplicity of activities on a continuous basis. Their minds are scattered, and they give superficial attention to what they are currently doing. Making a conscious decision to become a good listener, will indeed be challenging. We should therefore make a conscious and deliberate effort to listen with intent and be in the moment. Doing life together with others, is a communication intensive journey. The better we understand the other person's feelings and aspirations, the better the chance of them understanding our own feelings and aspirations. By so doing, we can co-create a common purpose. This will result in mutual respect, being comfortable to deal with conflict when it arises, enhanced influence, close companionship, and an improved quality of life. This feeds into your credibility construct.

The malicious pleasure of slander

What always baffles me, is this peculiar characteristic of human behaviour whereby most of us always find some sort of satisfaction and somehow become elated when we get reports of other people's mistakes, misfortunes, and weaknesses. We prefer to hear about the misfortune of others than of their accomplishments. We are more interested to hear some juicy account that puts someone in a bad light than something that is highly commendable about that person. What goes through your mind when someone, especially if he / she is a potential competitor in your space, experience some misfortune? Most of the time the natural inclination is towards expressing an exaggerated opinion to give it a negative slant, peddling half-truths and unsubstantiated speculations. The primary objective of these actions is to put the individual concerned in a less favourable position or sometimes it can even be very bold and blunt with the intention of damaging someone's reputation.

Many relationships have been shipwrecked because of indulging in this malicious pleasure. Slander starts very subtle but like slow poison, it can have a devastating effect on healthy personal relationships. Trust is very fragile and once it has been broken, it is exceedingly difficult to restore. We therefore have a responsibility to handle the good name and reputation of others with extreme care in the same manner that we expect ours to be preserved. Credible leaders are not repositories for slander and malicious rumours; that is a no-go area for them.

We have absolutely no control of what people might think and say about us, but we do have control over how we are going to respond to it. Slander and the possible offense it normally fosters, is like bait; if we fall for it, we go down with it hook, line and sinker. It really amazes me how many people I encounter daily who have been offended in some way or the other. When engaging in conversation, they usually wait for an opportunity to ventilate the issue that triggered the offence. Regrettably, we are living in a world with quite a few fragile egos. Offence can be a great source of annoyance, displeasure, and anger.

All of us will at some time be put to the test when being hurt by other's malicious intent. Before you respond – first recognise the offense for what it is. Was it done intentionally or was it merely a misunderstanding? Do not just react instinctively but first reflect before you act. Before you go off on a slandering excursion, have you shared your concerns with the other person directly. As indicated earlier, confrontation is not a swear word. In approaching the other person ask yourself "What is it that I want to achieve?" Do I want to seek vengeance, retribution, an opportunity to expose and shame or do I want to seek clarity, restoration, correction of a wrong and deepening of a relationship? Let me hasten to say, your approach might not necessarily result in a constructive resolution. You can either retaliate and hurt others in the process, simply ignore it or at best deal with it before the Lord. The latter is the safest; it takes grace to process the effects of our hurts and afflictions. I know it is not always that easy. I have been in such situations before where I humbled myself and the other party did not see the reason for reconciliation. You must determine in your heart that you are not going to continue talking about it, have a pity party about it or cuddle and feed your hurts. Bitterness and resentment will rob you of your joy in life.

I do not know about you but there are times in my life when I walked away from an encounter that was not pleasant, yet the scene keeps replaying itself in my mind. You almost rehearse in your mind that given another opportunity, what are the things which you would still have liked to say and the things that you would still love to do. It is almost like scripting a movie in your mind and every time you think about the incident, there is a new storyline being added. Does this sound familiar? My advice to you is turn off the movie in your mind. Life is just too short to be continuously occupied with he or she said or this one did this, and the other did that. Switch off that movie of offence! Have the bigger picture in mind. It is the small foxes that destroy the vineyard.

Wherever there is human interaction, there is absolutely no exemption from offense and hurts occasioned by malicious slander. May God grant us the grace not to delight in the misfortunes of others but always rejoice in their successes and good fortune. There is a good side in every person, and we must not allow that one incident adversely define the relationship. May we always see the good in others and seek as far as possible to live in harmony with one another. Slander kills!

Becoming fluent in the language of silence

Our country has indeed been blessed with such a rich cultural diversity. South Africa has eleven official languages and I always marvel at some of my friends that have the mastery of sometimes six to eight of our languages. It is still one of my biggest regrets that I have not invested more time in being fluent in at least a few more indigenous languages.

The other day, while attending one of the programmes I am enrolled for, one of my classmates made a remark that really caught my attention. She said that she was not very fluent in words and different languages, but one thing was for certain, she was very fluent in silence. The significance of this remark brought me to the realisation that one of the maladies of our times is the compulsive need for an adrenaline rush, informed by the desire for instant and quick fixes. Being quiet and just listening attentively, has become a lost art. The world is an extremely busy place with a myriad of activities and a never-ending buzz. If we could all develop a mastery in the language of silence, we will be more effective in whatever we do. We are an action driven society and let me hasten to say, there is nothing wrong about it. However, in our compulsion to respond to all manner of competing voices with its many contradictions, we normally lose our objectivity. This could be averted if we spend our time listening and reflecting to offer a well-considered response. Quietness and solitude are definitely not part of our modern-day lexicon.

Why are we afraid to unplug? I think the major reason is that we fear silence and solitude will unmask the truth about ourselves. We then devise all manner of escape mechanisms and try to drown the voice of our conscience with unwarranted activities. It might just be, that in your moment of silent reflection you will have to make uncomfortable decisions like ending a toxic relationship with someone you thought that you love and care about, forgiving someone that hurt you badly, dealing with pride, unsubstantiated envy and professional jealousy, owning up for negligence in your primary family relations, breaking a habit you might find enjoyable yet can be detrimental to your well-being, for example an extramarital relationship, pornography, gambling and the like.

We are also hesitant to enter the realm of solitude because it disarms us of the power to be seen and heard and our instructions complied with. It is in moments of solitude that my conscience asks the questions and not me calling the shots. We like to feel in-charge, hence silence and solitude make us feel vulnerable.

There is strength in silence. Be silent in the heat of anger when you do not have all the facts or verified the story. Be silent when you want to venture an opinion on matters that are none of your business and in the process inadvertently offend somebody. Do not feel obligated to respond to every question or challenge thrown at you. Some fights are not worth pursuing because you might win a battle but ultimately lose the war. This attitude speaks of credibility and a centred soul. The most precious moments are usually disguised in the simple things in life. We will miss out on these very life enriching experiences if we do not stop, look, listen and reflect.

There are so many things that constantly vie for our attention. These things sometimes inhibit our ability to distinguish noise from substance. May I kindly recommend that you spend at least one day per month (or even half a day) in a quiet place without any clutter; no television, newspapers, cell phone, laptop, Facebook, Instagram, whatever...OFF! It will surprise you how refreshing it is to clear your mind and reflect without any distractions. Silence reminds us that life still goes on without us.

You can also become a CEO

I still have a vivid picture in my mind of the early stages when I was appointed as the Chief Executive Officer (CEO) of a company for the first time. It was quite a mixed bag of excitement on the one hand, but equally overwhelming when I realised the enormity of the task in turning the business around. As a CEO you must be an embodiment of vision, inspiration, and aspiration. Over the years through God's grace, I was favoured with quite a few very influential leadership positions in my career. At this stage of my life, I have now consciously taken on a new CEO position – that of Chief Encouragement Officer.

As I interact with people daily, it is quite alarming how many of them are burdened with a sense of hopelessness, despondency and despair, desperately in need of encouragement. Encouragement is about inspiring, upliftment, giving confidence and hope. The opposite is discouragement, whereby one loses the desire and motivation to continue doing something that brings purpose and satisfaction in one's life. Discouragement has the nasty habit of just barging into your world. It steals your joy, cripples your confidence, and distorts the way you see yourself.

One must come to the realisation that people will disappoint you. You will also at times disappoint people and you might even disappoint yourself occasioned by the wrong choices you have made. Circumstances over which you have absolutely no control, may suddenly rock your world. The choice of giving up or going on, is the defining moment in your life.

One of the greatest attributes of leadership, is the ability to identify potential and attach value to it. The gift of encouragement is a deliberate and conscious action of giving someone confidence, inspiration and support. Encouragement is rooted in hope; a confident trust in something much bigger than your deepest fears.

How to be effective as a Chief Encouragement Officer:

1. Understand the bigger picture: You and I are placed on this earth to execute a higher purpose. Do you understand the higher purpose of your business, profession or role in life?
2. Walk in relational integrity: Meaningful engagement is a matter of trust. In this regard we all need someone that will accept us for who we are without being judgemental. When we are in each other's company we can be vulnerable because of the high level of trust. When we do not walk in relational integrity, Larry Crabb states it so aptly *"We will be known as reliable, but not involved. Honest friends will report that they enjoy being with us but have trouble feeling close. Even our spouses will feel guarded around us; a little tense and vaguely distant."* [43]
3. Active listening: A person's feelings and emotions cannot just be wished away. It must be dealt with and never be suppressed or discounted. Everyone has a story in life that needs to be respected and validated. Sometimes the individual just wants an opportunity to be listened to uninterruptedly; that in itself can be very therapeutic.
4. Model encouragement yourself: You can only give what you have. It is therefore important to cultivate a sense of self-awareness.

> What do I mean by that? It is your ability to notice your feelings, reactions, habits, behaviours, and thoughts. It is also about being cognisant of how it has an impact on those in your immediate sphere of influence. Self-awareness is being honest with yourself.

Are you really ready for the position of CEO? Being a Chief Encouragement Officer is intentional. Do not wait for that spectacular moment; start right where you are. Opportunities present themselves daily in your immediate environment. Make it a lifestyle to always have a positive disposition towards others. Never underestimate how that phone call, kind gesture, compliment, word of affirmation, constructive feedback or simply devoting time to lend a listening ear, can change someone's life.

Let the CEO in you show up!

I trust that you will appreciate how vital effective communication is to maintain your credibility. You cannot be found on the side of deception; how hard you try to spin it away. Always representing the facts truthfully, will enhance your credibility. People will respect you when you do not shy away from engaging in difficult conversations. It is not about me versus you, it is about us confronting a problem that threatens our relationship or organisational cohesiveness. This is approached with specific rationale, processes, and appropriate engagement towards a favourable outcome. Great leaders also learn not only to what is said but they also learn to discern the non-verbal cues. Equally important, they unplug to reflectively listen to the inner voice. I trust that what we have covered here will set you on a path towards effective communication and enhance your credibility.

PITSTOP

As mentioned earlier, I was appointed as CEO of the South African Bureau of Standards on 14 June 2004. I received a briefing from the Chief Financial Officer who was the Acting CEO before my arrival at about 08h00 the Monday morning and at 10h00, I had to address my first staff meeting. When I entered, the hall was packed to capacity, and one could sense the levels of anticipation on the faces of the staff. It felt as if it was a Presidential inauguration speech because there was a change of guard. The CFO tried her best to engage with the audience about the journey they traversed and the announcement of Cabinet regarding my appointment the previous Wednesday. As I observed the audience, I could not really gauge what was going on in their minds as they just gave her a cold and indifferent stare. They wanted to hear what this new fellow had to say.

It was ultimately my time to ascend the podium and there was just a prompting within in me to give my testimony. After a few pleasantries and introductory comments, they started to warm up. I told them the story of my life. A life informed by struggle and obscurity to one of great success. I then flipped the subject onto something that I knew most of the audience had a keen interest in. It is no secret that the majority of South African's are very passionate about soccer. One of the best supported teams is Kaizer Chiefs but let me hasten to say that I am a diehard Orlando Pirates supporter, their biggest rivals. Just a few months before my arrival, Kaizer Chiefs had just won the league for the first time in the history of the Premier Soccer League. They always showed great promise, at times winning a knockout cup but the league title eluded them for many years. They hired the late Ted Dimitriu as their coach, reinforced the team with some quality players and won the league. How did this relate to my work at hand?

I made them aware that SABS is a great institution with a very proud tradition. They used to be the apex quality institution in the country with a championship pedigree. For some reason or the other, they lost their winning streak and the trophy cabinet was empty. Instead, SABS had become known in the public eye for all the wrong reasons except winning accolades. Their shareholder, just like the owners of Kaizer Chiefs, decided to hire me as their coach to turn the fortunes of the institution around. I spelt out what they could expect of me as their coach and what I expected from them as my team players. I spelt it out as follows:

- I will be responsible for strategy, game tactics and team selection.
- Some of them that thought they are superstars, must earn their way into the starting line-up because there was a new game plan. Those that were benched for reasons not known to me, would make the squad if they proved themselves in training.

- Discipline was sacrosanct and all players would be treated equally and fairly.
- Player development was going to be one of my major focus areas and I committed to looking after the welfare of my players and create an environment in which they could excel.
- We needed to start winning games again and aim for trophies as that was the only way we were going to get our fans and possible sponsors back.
- We would run a profitable business that was well capacitated and would meet shareholder's expectations and regain our respect in the marketplace.

Informed by this metaphor, this is exactly how I approached my work over the ensuing five years. The message was broadcasted to staff members at all our different sites. This whole coach metaphor started to catch on very quickly. I was surprised during my very first visit to our Cape Town office during the question-and-answer session, most staff members addressed me as "Coach" instead of Mr Kuscus or CEO.

I discovered that there were talented people who were side- lined simply because they had fallen out of favour with the previous leadership. When I restructured the Commercial Division, I was able to appoint four highly qualified General Managers out of seven from previously disadvantaged backgrounds. However, I realised that although they were very good technical people, they were not so well versed in business development at a strategic level. I then headhunted a retired well experienced business executive John Stanbury for a three- year period to head up the Commercial Division. One of his KPI's was to groom his potential successor. Within two and a half years, John presented me with three top candidates. It was a marvel to see them in action during the interview process and to see the smooth handover of the baton between John Stanbury and Pravin Samnarian. The upward movement of some of the people who were just junior players were astounding. We introduced an incentive-based remuneration system that enhanced profitability and productivity. We did not have a single strike during my tenure because the rules of engagement were clearly defined.

People thrive under a vision that is compelling, persuasive, and inclusive. They need to see their role in the bigger scheme of things and need to be reassured that their contribution matters. There is nothing more powerful than a metaphor that people can be able to identify with. In my case the coach metaphor worked and when I left the SABS the results were there for all to see.

Chapter 9

MANNERS MATTER!

The revered African American scientist of the early 20th century George Washington Carver once said *"How far you go in life depends on your being tender with the young, compassionate with the aged, sympathetic with the striving and tolerant of the weak and strong. Because someday in your life you will have been all of these."* [44]

There is nothing more irritating than engaging with a leader who does not possess emotional intelligence. By emotional intelligence I mean the capacity to be aware of, control and express one's emotions and to handle interpersonal relationships with due care and sensitivity. It is that rare ability of a leader to demonstrate a level of maturity that even in the face of provocation, he or she becomes the anchor in stormy waters. To be credible as a leader, you have got to be centred in your soul. In marketing terms, they call it brand essence; those intangible emotions you want your customer to feel.

Those who lack credibility, often try to bolster their own image through loud and aggressive behaviour. They always want to be seen, heard, and acknowledged. They get easily agitated and distracted by peripheral issues. However, those that enjoy high levels of credibility always seem to be setting an appropriate mood, which is always conducive for meaningful engagement. Leaders with credibility are comfortable in their own skin and have a healthy regard for themselves and others.

Can you carry a full cup?

All of us who are in positions of leadership, need to be cognizant of the inherent temptation of seeking dominance and prominence in exercising authority. If left unchecked, we can lose focus on our primary leadership assignment and veer into areas such as manipulation, coercion, and victimisation of our followers. The effects can be catastrophic. Oswald Chalmers puts it so aptly *"Not everyone can carry a full cup. Sudden elevation frequently leads to pride and a fall."* [45]

How do you use power over those under your authority? Is there always this natural urge to remind them who is the boss? Do we squash those who disagree with us and dispense patronage to those who never question our actions regardless of how wrong it might be? Do I have the last say over every matter and do not even open up space and opportunity for others to think, make suggestions or plan with me? Are my follower's lives controlled by unspoken rules and people live under a constant threat of possible dismissal?

Half of the problems in the world are due to people who want to feel important. Lurking in the heart of every ego-centric leader, is the need to always occupy centre stage. These attributes start subtly and can later define the whole personality of the leader. The root of this problem is that leaders have an overestimation of their own importance and significance in comparison with others.

I was recently in an intense conversation with the owner of a very reputable financial services company regarding the toxic corporate culture that is becoming mainstream in certain sectors of the marketplace. This phenomenon has adverse consequences and its implications for value destruction is not yet fully appreciated. Very bright and promising professionals' careers are prematurely aborted, and energy is diverted into undue contestation instead of being applied to productive and beneficial output. I have no doubt that as you read this, you know at least one casualty in this scheme of things. There is a massive shake up in leadership throughout the world and South Africa has not been spared. The power game leaders play with their exaggerated sense of self-importance, is increasingly running out of options and cannot be sustained indefinitely.

The no-nonsense, all about the bottom-line, nothing is going to stop me kind of approach of leadership, has proven to be toxic and highly destructive.

Authority is developmental in nature. When exercising authority, the primary objective is to build people and not to destroy them. This is not a spineless, wishy washy type of leadership, subject to the whims and fancies of others. As a matter of fact, the greatest leaders inspire others to do the right thing whereas the worst leaders, force them into submission. People might grudgingly comply for a little while but in an environment devoid of mutual respect, they will find a way of striking back. In our day and age, we also have a more open society where people have access to all kinds of information to enhance their decision-making capability. With the advent of the digital age, any blunder by a leader can go viral on social media platforms. People can be very mean on these platforms and can put a leader in a very compromising position with enormous reputational consequences. It is therefore in the interest of any serious leader to exercise authority sensibly and sensitively. This is what a healthy composure is all about.

My philosophy in leadership has always been - the higher you go up in leadership, the less you should do. You need to adequately empower those reporting to you so that it can create sufficient margin of time for you to think ahead. You always need to be a few steps forward to position the organisation to be future fit and nurture those strategic relationships for business growth. A misplaced sense of authority can lead to a deceived sense of self-importance, informed by a distorted notion that if you leave your position, your organisation will not survive. The art of leadership is to lead yourself out of a job and reinvent yourself at a higher level, leveraging from your hard-earned learning experiences. It will also ensure that what you have worked so hard for, will be of an enduring nature. If you delegate with concomitant authority, you will broaden your leadership pipeline. Those reporting to you, will take co-ownership of the vision and diligently bring their creativity to bear to expand the vision far beyond what you could have accomplished in your lifetime.

There is no greater desire in my life then to see that the hard miles that I put into any endeavour, yield results way beyond my lifespan in the organisation. Therefore, whilst still being around, I need to stay humble; misplaced authority engenders pride and arrogance. There should always be a genuine concern for the people I have been entrusted to lead. It is so easy to make demands on people if you are in a position of authority. I should however be an embodiment of excellence and never demand what I have not been able to demonstrate myself to those in my team. As I go about my responsibilities, I must always treat my position like rented space and not as if I have a title deed to it. This will greatly assist me to discern when it is an appropriate time to move on. Some leaders get so intoxicated with authority that they overstay their brief with disastrous consequences.

Not everyone can handle authority sensibly and sensitively. To remain in the game, you will be well advised to develop high levels of emotional intelligence. I have seen and worked in my lifetime with very influential people, who ended up on the leadership scrapyard because of misguided and misplaced authority.

Can you carry a full cup?

Never underestimate the temptation to be "somebody"

There is something that always fascinates me when I go to social functions. During a personal introduction, the first set of questions asked normally revolves around "Where do you live? Which company do you work for? What is your title?" This immediately puts you in a kind of pecking order that sets the parameters for any further level of engagement. This notion is a function of status – our conscious or sometimes unconscious ranking or position in society in comparison to others.

One's desire for social status and acceptance can arguably be the most powerful force that drives behaviour. It is no secret that the higher your status or even perceived status in society, the better your chances to access special privileges, opportunities, rewards, recognition and just a more favourable disposition in the public eye. Social status is a key factor with major implications in our lives.

Regrettably, in a highly status conscious world, people became so entrapped in this phenomenon at the expense of authentic engagement. Obsession with a positive public profile, has caused many individuals to feed their vanity through a potent diet of pride, lust, deceit, power, and prestige. What also exacerbates the problem is a powerful media platform that elevates these artificial endeavours above what makes for genuine and meaningful living. There is nothing wrong with advancing in life. However, the litmus test is whether in your interaction with people, you consistently display appropriate and emotional health that sets a positive mood.

There is tremendous value in anonymity. Exceptional feats were accomplished by people from a position of relative obscurity. I thrive exceptionally well outside the limelight and fashioned my life along the lines of a boutique, just for the discerning and informed customer. People will know and appreciate the value that is on offer in a boutique unlike the bold “for sale” signs we find all over the place in some of the shopping centres. The virtues of modesty, privacy and humility have become the guiding principles in my engagement with the outside world. Pride informs the misplaced desire for undue attention. Acting with humility does not in any way mean you have to deny your self-worth but rather that you also consciously see the worth in others. It is all about taking on the heart of a servant and extending God’s love to those in need of it.

In John 13: 1 -17 Jesus demonstrated practically through washing his disciple’s feet, what it means to go against the grain of the status trap. Servanthood and stripping away of any tinge of ego, is the heart of great leadership. It is that conscious and deliberate choice of sacrificial service as opposed to the compulsive yearning to be a superstar.

Never underrate the temptation to be “somebody”. My prayer is that God will help us to steer away from the status trap and that we will frequently make an honest assessment on some of the following:

- Is my heart fully devoted to Him and Him alone?
- Am I genuinely connected or maintain a certain aloof distance from ordinary people? What kind of atmosphere do I create to set a positive mood in my interactions with others?
- To what extent did I allow the trappings of status to define the culture of the organisation I am leading and what needs to be done to reverse that paradigm?

Our greatest desire in life should be to ultimately know the Father's heart and out of that experience find the courage and strength to lead and influence our world in a manner that pleases Him; unfettered from the trappings of status. Wherever we go we should represent His presence that will be manifested through a healthy level of emotional intelligence that sets a positive mood.

The trap of overconfidence

I like golf and at some stage I used to play it quite often but nowadays I am just a social player. There are some great leadership lessons to be learned from the game and one of it is to maintain your composure on the course. I have often seen players become so upset with the way they play that they will throw their golf club into the water, scream some obscenity, and become just downright miserable to play with. Playing 18 holes can be a long and miserable walk if you are not enjoying what you are doing. Forget the bad shots and delight in the good ones.

One of the greatest golf players in history was the late Arnold Palmer. In recalling a lesson about overconfidence by this golfing legend, Carol Mann in an article The 19th Hole, wrote about it as follows:

"It was the final hole of the 1961 US Masters Golf Tournament, and I had a one-stroke lead and just hit a very satisfying tee shot. I felt I was in good shape. As I approached my ball, I saw an old friend of mine standing at the edge of the gallery. He motioned over, stuck out his hand and said Congratulations! I took his hand and shook it but as I did, I knew I had lost my focus. On my next two shots, I hit the ball into the sand trap, then over the edge of the green. I missed a putt and lost the Masters. You don't forget a mistake like that." [46]

A successful leader is an embodiment of genuine confidence regarding vision, how to accomplish it and how to navigate potential obstacles when it arises. He or she inspires followers into action to go on a journey which they have never been before. No one wants to be associated with a leader that suffers from low self-esteem. There is however a phenomenon called overconfidence, where the belief in one's ability is out of proportion to reality. It is a failure to collate factual information because you are too sure of your own assumptions. When you are overconfident, you misjudge your value, opinion, beliefs, and abilities. When you are deceived by overconfidence, your favourite response is "It will not happen to me."

Just like Arnold Palmer, we have all had episodes of overconfidence at some stage of our lives. We broke promises which we thought we could fulfil, said things as if it were the gospel, committed to something without factoring in our own constraints and thought we could pull it off, took on an assignment just to prove a point, went through a well-known routine without even having to think through it when suddenly, the unexpected happens.

At times, some of us can simply become too arrogant and comfortable with what we know and achieved and then completely lose touch with reality. In his book How Much is Enough, Andrew Bradley [47] describes how intelligent professionals like doctors, lawyers, engineers, and the like, can be notorious investors. They assume that success in their speciality will translate seamlessly into the complexity of the investment space. They simply do not take the time and effort to get to grips with market dynamics through specialist input. Past successes are no guarantee that we will be victorious in our current situation. We need to balance our past experiences with a serious dose of realism and a high degree of humility and vigilance.

One of the biggest driving forces of overconfidence is a narcissistic attitude. The word has its origin in Greek mythology, where the young Narcissus fell in love with his own image reflected in a pool of water. This attitude manifests itself in an overinflated sense of self-worth. Sometimes this can be used as a subtle defence mechanism for underlying personality deficits. A person who was not loved during childhood might try to win the love and attention from others through constant attention seeking. An under achiever in early life might like to compensate for lost ground and even buy his or her way into a position of prominence.

Pride is another driver of overconfidence where people feel obligated to upstage others. In most cases it is done out of egoistic considerations. It creates a situation where people have an obsession to receive acknowledgement for any work done, shuns inputs and correction from others, can even manipulate the facts to look good and others look bad for as long as they get the glory. Pride continuously sings the famous Frank Sinatra song "I did it my way."

I do quite a bit of public speaking assignments. One of the guiding principles in my approach in this regard, is to never underestimate my audience or take them for granted. I prepare well by immersing myself into the best possible resources available. I deliver well by giving it my all in a passionate, persuasive yet graceful manner. But beforehand, I also pray for God's divine enablement to transform the lives of my audience and for me to embrace the learning opportunities out of every encounter. The words of Paul in Romans 12: 3 (Amplified) is quite instructive in this regard "*... I warn everyone among you not to estimate and think of himself more highly than he ought, not have an exaggerated opinion of his own importance but to rate his ability with sober judgement...*"

With all the temptations, there are consequences if we succumb to overconfidence. It is therefore critical to frequently do a reality check in the mirror and address the real you by:

- Being honest with yourself and tracing the root cause why you had embarked on the hazardous path of overconfidence.
- Distinguishing fact from fiction. Some of our overconfident endeavours are pursued without interrogating the facts, weighing up alternatives or seeking expert opinion. We sometimes just plunge head-on into something because it massages our ego.
- Remaining focussed on the task at hand. Do not get intoxicated by the applause of the audience or seeking out the undue admiration of others. Beware of short cuts by manipulating people to boost your profile, it can be costly in the long run.
- Committing to things you can pull off. Do not pretend to be MacGyver. Major in your strengths and do not get embroiled into competing with others out of selfish considerations.
- Appreciating and celebrating your true identity. You are unique in many ways; start to embrace it, excel in it and establish yourself as a brand in your area of expertise without being envious of what you don't have.

The best antidote for overconfidence is to walk in humility. It is not about a low self-image but a healthy and measured view of self. Pride and overconfidence are pathological and come with a high premium. Humility brings you to the realisation that all you have accomplished, accumulated, or achieved, is only by God's grace. When we acknowledge Him as the Source, it brings out the best in us because we know that it is not about us, it is about Him. Remain centred in your soul!

The eye of the storm

Typhoons are violent rotating storms. They occur mostly in the western Pacific and Indian oceans. Given the hot and humid temperatures in these regions, surface water heats up causing rapid evaporation. As the hot air rises, it is replaced by cold air leading to massive swirling cloud formations. In the process, wind velocity picks up reaching speeds of up to 200 km per hour, leaving a trail of destruction in its path. Through modern satellite imaging and related advancements in the meteorological sciences, formation of a typhoon can be picked up long before it erupts. It all starts with what is termed the eye, a calm region at the centre of the storm.

Similarly, in our own lives things may look normal and peaceful from a distance, yet there is trouble and strife looming. If it is not picked up timeously, it might have devastating consequences. Maintaining high levels of emotional intelligence, requires that we take cognisance of the warning signals that can throw our composure totally out of balance. Some of the signals that are indicative of a looming storm brewing on the inside include mood swings where you have sporadic bursts of anger, prolonged bouts of sadness and a continuing sense of irritability. Other signals include sleeplessness, guilt, lack of focus, defensiveness, and highly suspicious attitudes.

I would specifically like to focus on a signal that is becoming very pervasive in our country and that is anger. By all indications, South Africa is a terribly angry society. One only has to travel on the highways during peak traffic to witness the impatience, irritability and at times downright rudeness which in certain instances may end up in road rage. The increasing levels of Gender Based Violence depicts a story of the anger of men in our society that knows no bounds. One just needs to look at the destructive effects of "peaceful" protest action where valuable infrastructure like classrooms, libraries and government offices are gutted because demands were not met.

There is a potential tsunami in all of us. The intense demands of modern life can become a vicious cycle. Burnout causes inefficiency; inefficiency creates increasing demands and demands create pressure and concomitant guilt for not achieving desired goals. Added pressure and guilt causes stress, stress causes depleted energy and drive which leads to burnout, which leads to inefficiency.... The cycle goes on and on until it gains velocity and develops into a full - blown storm with devastating consequences.

Just as meteorologists constantly monitor satellite images for cyclonic activities, so must we constantly reflect on our own lives. Reflection is that ability to stop and look inside of ourselves and ask honest questions in an attempt to give genuine and sincere responses. It should be authentic in nature and address the critical question: "What is my soul saying to me?" Never become too busy for yourself. Some people try to evade the hard questions and drown the voice of their soul by filling their lives with endless activity, noise, and meaningless engagements. Silence intimidates them.

My reflection might range from issues such as what is the significance of recent events in my life? How do I relate to key people in my life? What triggered my current lack of focus, enthusiasm, and passion on my journey of life? Why this sudden sense of desperation to prove myself to others? What are the deepest fears that are currently pre-occupying my mind? Through reflective thinking, I can draw from my reservoir of past life experiences and zoom into those aspects that gave me peace of mind. This greatly assists me to gain a fresh perspective on sometimes extraordinarily complex issues and the necessary strength to move forward.

To proactively deal with the potential anger tsunami:

- Throw away the crutches. Do not use your anger as a defence mechanism to mask underlying insecurities. Deal with it.
- Think before you speak. In the heat of the moment, it is easy to say something which you will later regret.

- Own up and do not play the blame game. If I worked somewhere else, if it wasn't for the government, if my parents did not, if my spouse could only....
- Agree to disagree. Some battles are not worth winning at all costs.

Continuous reflection will help us to timeously identify what is wrong and needs to be corrected. It helps us to assess what are the necessary preparations to be made and what assistance needs to be mobilised before the storm hits our shores.

Control your emotions before your emotions control you!

A blind spot called subjectivity

Navigating through peak hour traffic on the busy highways of Johannesburg, especially during the rainy season, can be a daunting task. The unpredictability of a mini-bus taxi driving in front of you or the weaving of motorbikes in between lanes, awakens the Lewis Hamilton within me. One should always be in a state of high alert about blind spots. What do I mean with a blind spot? A blind spot in a vehicle refers to an area around the vehicle that cannot be observed by the driver whilst driving, under existing circumstances.

Just like in driving, in our leadership journey, there might be things that can cause great harm and might even be fatal, if we do not react to it timeously. If not attended to, these entrenched patterns of thinking and behaving (admittedly, sometimes unknown to us) can negatively influence the way in which we relate to other people.

The nature of my work in the corporate world, very often places me at the centre of having to mediate amidst strong opposing viewpoints from different constituencies or individuals in an organisation. This may range from destructive conflict among senior executives, non-performance on agreed objectives, misalignment of expectations between different stakeholders, strategies to enhance business growth in a downward cycle or sometimes sheer petty company politics. The intensity of some of these engagements can at times tax my composure to its limits.

Let me clarify and state that I have a genuine appreciation for diversity of views. It enriches our decision- making process and creates opportunities for mutual growth and development. I am also a strong believer that team members must be allowed to differ without being labelled or victimised for holding a different view. Unlike robots, human beings are not programmed to give a predictable response. We all have unique perspectives about life, and it is therefore perfectly normal to differ at times.

To respond to the daunting challenge of reconciling opposing views, every leader must have two critical skills in his or her armoury, that is tact and diplomacy. Tact comes from the same root word for tactile, which denotes touch. Leaders must therefore deal with others in difficult situations with due care and sensitivity. Likewise, leaders should master the art of diplomacy; helping individuals or interest groups to get along and work harmoniously for the common good. This requires a high degree of sensibility which come from the Latin word sensibilis, meaning showing good sense, being reasonable and exercising sound judgement. Oswald Saunders says the following in this regard *"Leaders need to be able to reconcile opposing viewpoints without giving offense or compromising principle. A leader should be able to project into the life and heart and mind of another, then setting aside personal preferences, deal with the other in a fashion that fits the other best."* [48]

I always think of myself as a very objective person. However, on a few occasions I had to grapple with the naked reality of some of my hidden prejudices and cultural preferences. We all see the world through the lens of our own socialisation, past life experiences and value system. However, what we should be vigilant about, is that our objectivity must not be clouded to the extent that it leads to favouritism, unsubstantiated bias, and even subtle discrimination. Objectivity demands from all of us, that we deal with the factual situation and exercise rational judgement unfettered by emotions and personal prejudices.

As leaders, one of our major responsibilities revolves around decision making. We must therefore be mindful of all those subjective aspects in our personality construct which can have a strong bearing on our judgement. If left unchecked, it can become a blind spot resulting in patterns of thinking, feeling, and behaving we do unconsciously, that will negatively influence our relationship with other people.

There are times when we can be so wrong in being right. This stems from a lack of measured composure. It is not always the correctness of your assumptions and arguments that matter. What is of critical importance, is the way you communicate it. We can be persuasive, precise, and compelling in getting our point of view across but in the process hurt someone or inflicts his / her dignity. It is not always the easiest thing to do to speak hard truths in a measured and composed way into the lives of others. It all boils down to the motives of our heart. Our primary motives should always be towards restoration and not destruction, care and not indifference, encouragement and not discouragement and affirmation not disqualification. By doing this, we are not necessarily compromising on matters of principle but out of a sincere desire to see a convergence of the original purpose notwithstanding the extent of veering off course.

May I raise with you this critical question. How objective are you in your decision making and what are the prejudices, bias and preferences that sometimes cloud your objectivity? What practical steps will you take to deal with it?

PITSTOP

There are some decisions in life that have long-term implications and should be well considered. There were two such decisions in my life; the woman I was going to marry and the first property I bought. The first one was a question of a commitment until death do us part and the second one, comes with a bond of at least 20 years. You can imagine the excitement for Liz and I when we moved into our first house in 1988. The finances were approved by the bank, we had already moved into the house and were just awaiting final registration of the property at the Deeds Office when out of the blue we were hit by a massive setback. I was told by the lawyers who dealt with the registration, that the Deeds Office had declined the registration. This really rattled my cage.

There was a very ugly piece of legislation from the apartheid regime called the Group Areas Act of 1950. This act assigned racial groups to different residential and business sections in urban areas. According to this law, one racial group could not stay in the designated area of another. If a Black person was found to be residing in a White area, he or she would be imprisoned and charged with a serious criminal offense. The same applied for Coloureds and Indians.

As mentioned earlier, Alabama where we lived was a designated Coloured area and my wife Liz is of Tswana origin. By virtue of us having been married in community of property, Liz became a joint owner in the property and in terms of this apartheid Group Areas Act, she was forbidden to exercise that right. It really felt so insulting and dehumanising to us and our marriage. All our dreams and ideas of how we were going to turn the place around and create a haven for our children to thrive and develop, just seemed like a pipedream.

My first port of call was the local township manager's office to acquaint myself with the facts. There I was met by a guy called Gert. The township manager's position was always occupied by Afrikaner men who were generally ultra-conservative and great enforcers of the apartheid statutes and means of control. When I entered this manager's office, he made me to sit down. After I explained to him the reason for coming to see him, he lit up his pipe. He then took me very slowly through each article of this abhorrent piece of apartheid legislation, clause by clause and line by line. Just the tone of his voice could not hide the fact that this man was delighting in rubbing salt in my wounds. He would punctuate his reading with "Dit is wat die wet se" (this is what the law says, and I cannot do anything about it.) and lurking behind this, was a clear indication of who was the boss. I listened to him in a cool, calm and collected manner and the political activist in me kept his emotions in check.

Out of desperation, I consulted two lawyers, and both gave me the same advice. To circumvent this legislative roadblock, I was advised to divorce my wife and then remarry out of community of property. Divorce my wife? Even that carried certain risks. Based on the laws of that time, if I had to die, my wife would have to sell the house and she and my children would have to get alternative accommodation in a Black township. This really felt like a millstone around my neck. This was also a time when our marriage was flourishing. At that time when this challenge hit us, we were attending a 14- week Marriage Enrichment Course at Rhema Church in Orkney every Monday night. We were seriously investing in our marriage relationship and the suggestion of a divorce caught us off-balance. We really prayed about this situation like never before. I had to be strong for my family during this challenging time and tried at best, to set a positive mood. I did not dare allow us to wallow in despair.

One evening while sitting and chatting with Liz about this elephant in the room, a brainwave just hit me. I decided to beat the system with the system. My class teacher in matric John Douw, was a member of the Coloured Representative Council, some apartheid structure in the Tricameral Parliamentary System. Though John Douw and I were on the opposite sides of the political spectrum, I respected him as a person. He knew very well that I abhorred his collaboration with the apartheid regime. I arranged a meeting with him one Saturday afternoon and he was furious when I explained to him my story of naked discrimination. To his credit, he went right up to the then Minister of Home Affairs to present my case and that same week, an order was immediately issued for the reclassification of Liz as a Coloured. It remains a big joke amongst us about how the official at the local Home Affairs office told Liz that she has to abandon her beautiful second name Keolebogile (which means - thank you in Setswana) because it does not sound like a Coloured name. Till today she is only Elizabeth Kuscus. Even the classification amongst Coloureds was another joke. Esther, Ezra and I are classified as Cape Coloured, Liz is classified Other Coloured and Zoe a South African. What a joke of a system was this apartheid monster?

After a delay of about six months, the house was eventually registered in our names. It sounds so strange to tell this story and we still have a big laugh about it when we reflect on those days. But let me hasten to say, the very foundation of our union was brought into question by the apartheid laws. Our dignity inflicted by the Gert's of this world and the risks to the future of my family in the event of me dying, was heavy on my mind. By the grace of God, we are still married for 39 years now. We also had the privilege to later register other properties in our name, without the hassles of the Group Areas Act.

Why am I taking this route with you? For the younger generation, we come from a very unfortunate apartheid past; some of its effects are still with us. We should never forget where we come from and take our political freedom for granted. This was a painful experience for Liz and me but instead of making us bitter, it made us better. In the final analysis love conquered it all. Let me also mention, that when you are confronted with a challenge or setback in life, do not make hasty and expedient decisions and allow your emotions to run ahead of you. Evaluate all your options carefully; the first set of advice might not necessarily be the best option. Do not play into the hands of your adversary, notwithstanding the height of provocation. Emotional intelligence dictates that you maintain your composure and make sound and carefully considered decisions.

Chapter 10

THE RHYTHM OF CONSISTENCY

A rhythm is a regular, repeated movement or sound. When you think of the rhythm of a wall clock, our heartbeat or pulse, our breathing, the rising of the sun in the morning; we are reminded that all these examples carry an element of regularity and predictability. If these rhythms stop, it leads to dysfunctionality and may even be life threatening.

We are living in a highly diversified world where people are spoilt for choice. If one just thinks of the many mobile devices on the market, different models of cars, clothing labels, career options, restaurants and food outlets, television channels, recreational activities and even churches to name but a few. We are also bombarded with massive amounts of advertisements where a multitude of product or service offerings compete for our attention on a continuous basis. It is sometimes rather difficult for one to decide between various options because the differential is sometimes negligible and at first glance, looks equally appealing and attractive.

One distinguishing characteristic for the future survival of a product or service is the principle of consistency. Consistency denotes the quality of always behaving or performing in a similar fashion, maintaining the same standards, being stable, reliable, and dependable. Consistency brings about an element of predictability where there is always an expectation of a particular type of performance. At an organisational level, it can have the effect of transforming it to something outstanding. At a personal level, consistency can propel your credibility from being ordinary and mediocre to being excellent and phenomenal. Anthony Robbins describes it as *"It's not what we do once in a while that shapes our lives. It's what we do consistently"* [49] There should be a rhythm in all your key endeavours. It gives one a sense of coherence so that there are no contradictions in what people experience about you at any given point in time. Society is yearning for consistency especially in our leadership echelons. There are just too many instances where we see leaders vacillate from one position to the other on matters of principle, conduct, decision making and public pronouncements.

Consistency is about longevity; you are in it for the long haul. Consistency acts as an inspiration not only to our peers but also for generations to come. They will be able to realise that you have proven yourself to be resilient notwithstanding the challenges that life threw at you. You need to be known as someone that went through the eye of the needle, being tried and tested, having weathered the storms. Your life is not only about the spotlight and fleeting moments of bliss. It extends right down to the engine room and proverbial trenches. You need to know how to embrace victory as well as moving forward with courage in moments of defeat. Your consistency will even make it easy for others to follow and trust you to take them into areas that they might not have explored in their lives before. Consistency will show you to be credible, someone that can be believed and trusted.

Consistency has an enduring attraction and is powerful. In the words of Osho Samuel Adetunji *"If you can strike the chord of consistency on the guitar of your life, the world will dance to your music of greatness."* [50] Before you devote yourself to a leader, it is important to ask hard and critical questions about consistency on how the leader conducts him or herself. Conversely, if you aspire to be a credible leader whose example is worth emulating, it will be worthwhile to invest your time and energy on those aspects that will enable you to maintain high standards of consistency at all times.

Are you willing to put your signature on the line?

In my professional life, my signature is often required to validate the contents of a document. Sometimes it is a single page and at times I virtually must read through quite a volume of pages, initial each one of them and append my final signature onto the document. Most of us have at some stage signed a document without meticulously going through the total contents. A signature on a document signifies knowledge, approval and acceptance or obligation. A signature is also evidence of the origin and intentions of the affected parties.

A signature does not only represent your name but also a reflection of values, honour, and the totality of what you stand for. It is a commitment to adhere to a certain set of standards and the implications are huge. One can imagine the consequences if a medical doctor signs off on a wrong prescription and the patient dies because of a drug overdose.

During my tenure as CEO of the South African Bureau of Standards, I came to appreciate the value of my signature. As a third- party certification body, once the quality mark was put on a product and I had signed the certificate, it implied that the product or service had been tested and verified to the highest standards of quality; it was safe and fit for purpose. On a few occasions, unscrupulous business operators fraudulently presented themselves as mark holders and we had to embark on very tight controls and sophisticated measures to safeguard the integrity of the processes.

In life, each day we live is a signature day. It is an expression of the values we espouse and the honour with which we would like to engage with the issues at hand on that particular day. It is about a conscious awareness that each day is a gift from our Creator and we've got to embrace both the positive and negative and give it our best shot. It is about going to bed at night knowing that you maximised the opportunities that came your way, seized the valuable moments of learning, and did not succumb to expediency but remained principled. Marilyn Carlson Nelson the CEO of Carlson Companies puts this whole notion of making the most of each day so succinctly *"Are you willing to put your signature on this day?"* [51]

What will be your honest response to the question "Is my life in absolute good shape or am I limping from episode to episode without any fulfilment and no joy at all?"

The ultimate source of joy and contentment regardless of the circumstances, is rooted in the Lord. Sometimes we ascribe too much credit to our own skills set, intellect, personality, and networks. Let me categorically state that it has everything to do with our Creator because in Him we live and move and have our being. If we maintain a cohesive relationship with the Lord and in a disciplined manner remain in communion with Him, we will live an over-flowing life.

It sometimes happens that power of attorney is conferred on an individual(s) to sign on behalf of someone else or an organisation. Legally, this authority can only be granted to a person considered to be fit and proper. The concept of a fit and proper person is a fundamental one in many professions, jurisdictions and organisations as it is used to determine a person's honesty, integrity and reputation in order to confirm that they are fit and proper for the role they are undertaking. Your Creator holds you in high esteem. He has endowed you with the requisite capabilities and regards you as a fit and proper person for a specific assignment in life. As we go about our lives, we must always remember that we operate under delegated authority on behalf of our Creator.

We should therefore be mindful about the implications of all our actions as we go about our lives. Our primary responsibility is to validate the principles of His Kingdom on a consistent basis and be an embodiment of His character in all we do. Anything less than that will be a fraudulent signature and may open us up for adverse consequences. My prayer is that God grant you and I the grace that at the end of each day, we will be able to appropriately respond to this critical question "Am I willing to put my signature on this day?"

When trust has been betrayed

Trust is one of the most essential attributes that defines us as human beings. Trust is like the rhythmic heartbeat of any human interaction. If there is no trust, there will be no meaningful relationship. The word trust denotes a firm belief and confidence about the reliability, truth, and strength of someone or something. Credible leaders display the latter qualities on a consistent basis. To say that we have a huge trust deficit in our society, is an understatement. This has an inhibiting effect on our ability to engage meaningfully with each other and craft coherent responses to the challenges that need our collective effort. We have a crisis of trust in government, the education system, health care delivery, the financial system, marriage, and family life (not forgetting Eskom). There is deep mistrust towards the corporate world by labour and vice versa.

Leaders should never lose sight of the higher purpose that informs the existence of institutions they are leading. This should never be exchanged for short-term initiatives borne out of self-interest. Our country comes from a very unfortunate past with the socio-economic challenges we have been bequeathed, still stubbornly abiding with us. We were blessed by the innate values of the founding fathers of our new democratic dispensation. Their consistency in upholding impeccable values and consistently occupying the moral high ground, had to a large extent shaped a constitutional order premised on equality and service above self. Regrettably, too many in our leadership ranks betrayed the trust and confidence instilled in us by our founding fathers and the expedient abandonment of values have reached crisis proportions. In my observation, the major causative factor that systematically exacerbated the trust deficit in society is a loss of perspective on the higher purpose of leadership.

I think that you will agree with me that we have the potential to become a great country again and hold our own amongst the community of nations. On many occasions, we have already demonstrated our capability in this regard. We all have a responsibility to take collective stewardship at all levels of society to decisively narrow the trust deficit. Without trust, our country will not reach the optimal potential or experience a higher quality of life together as a nation. What can you and I do in our various spheres of influence to rebuild trust amongst ourselves at an individual, institutional and broader societal level?

1. It all starts at the top. There is a famous Chinese proverb that says, "The fish rots from the head." Likewise, if we want to reverse the

downward trend and establish trust on a consistent level, it will have to start with all of us who are occupying leadership positions in our various spheres of influence. Our followers must be able to trust us as we walk the talk on a consistent basis. John Maxwell once stated that there are three simple questions every follower asks of a leader:

- Do you care for me? (Compassion)
- Can I trust you? (Character)
- Can you help me? (Competence) [52]

2. Trusteeship: Leaders need to be mindful of the implications their actions might have on generations to come. We do not own our positions of authority; we are merely trustees and must act in the best interest of the beneficiaries.
3. Authentic communication. By this I mean that our words, actions, and attitudes must be truthful. If we deny or even withhold truth, we are living in deception.
4. Grace. Developing trust is a process and takes time and effort. Always be gracious in your engagement and be open to the views of others in your team.
5. Celebration. Be grateful for every milestone reached on this journey and never neglect an opportunity to affirm those that made it happen.

Trust is fragile; handle it with care. Like a cracked vase, we might put all the pieces together with Super Glue, but it will never be the same again. There are definite rewards for being trustworthy on a consistent basis. Never underestimate your contribution in ensuring that the trust levels are enhanced in your sphere of influence. God sees it and will reward you in due season.

Facts are your best friend

Consistency in decision making, is one of the defining features of a credible leader. I serve on a few company Boards and quite a considerable amount of my time is spent in meetings. The ultimate objective of a meeting is to arrive at qualitative decisions. Qualitative decisions are based on qualitative information. Some of these decisions can be quite weighty and might range from issues such as considering a new strategic direction for the company, applying our minds to a complex legal matter that might put the company at risk, acquainting ourselves with new emerging trends that can erode the company's profitability or unblocking unforeseen and unavoidable impediments that stall progress on strategic projects. Over the years I had to learn the art of meticulously distilling the objective facts in these Board meetings. By so doing I was able to consistently fulfil my fiduciary responsibilities appropriately.

It never fails to amaze me how certain people can complicate things when reporting on a matter in meetings. It almost seems as though they prefer everything to be clouded in volumes of unrelated detail so that you cannot drill down to the essentials. One sometimes get a sense that there is a subtle attempt to create barriers so that others are not exposed to the whole truth. Maybe you have also been at some stage in a difficult situation where facts were not necessarily your strong point and the fear of you being projected as a failure, clouded your judgement. My honest advice to you based on hard earned experience, is regardless of how unpalatable it might be, always embrace the facts as your best friend. Everybody is entitled to an opinion, but nobody has the right to alter the facts.

By objectively presenting the facts, you will be freed up from the stranglehold of fear and develop the necessary confidence in engaging with your colleagues towards an appropriate solution. In addition, by embracing the facts, you can plan better, enhance your decision-making capability and move forward with a higher degree of certainty. This will enhance your credibility as your contribution will be sound and well considered.

I am a firm believer that there are always three sides to a story: your side, the other person's side, and the truth. The latter is based on objective facts. I can recall the many times people "took me into their confidence" about concerns they had about what was happening in other colleague's lives. On closer scrutiny, I discovered that the person's report was at serious variance with the factual situation. In most cases it was informed by malicious intent or self-interest. It is rather regrettable that in today's highly competitive environment, people will stoop to character assassination, in pursuit of self-promotion at someone else's expense. There were so many times in my life that I was wrongly briefed about someone, only later to discover a different side of that person. Never allow your objectivity to be clouded in your interaction with someone based solely on the account of others. Acquaint yourself with the facts through your own experience with the individual, to arrive at an appropriate conclusion. We all carry scars and wounds of misguided opinions held about us, informed by a distorted set of facts.

Life is already very overbearing and complicated. People are constantly looking for straightforward and simple answers that will make a difference in their lives. If you want to be regarded as a credible depository of solutions then you must remain current, simple, and factual. Do not create exaggerated expectations; people will soon see through the facades. You may have heard of spin-doctors. This is a thriving industry. Its practitioners are skilled in constructing responses to pressing questions, with the sole purpose of concealing the facts. Regrettably, a lie gets legs and cannot be contained indefinitely. Instead of wasting precious time and energy to "spin" a story, rather be upfront with the facts. Face the challenge head-on and direct your time and energy to communicate a solution-oriented narrative.

Also be very careful about generalisations. Many leaders have caused untold damage by conveniently distorting the facts to enhance their narrow perspective. They can so easily fall into the trap of making sweeping statements to sustain their narrative. Their favourite cliches being "you always, you never, you forever..." My friend, stick to the facts!

It serves no purpose at all to deal with peripheral matters and paper the cracks. In colloquial terms "cut to the chase." If you really have my wellbeing at heart, you will constructively engage with me based on facts about what the real problem is. This will avert a similar occurrence moving forward. Love should always be the primary motivator for any remedial action as opposed to naming, blaming, and shaming.

> *"Get the facts or the facts will get you. And when you get them, get them right, or they will get you wrong."* (Dr Thomas Fuller) [53]

Tomorrow is today

One of the biggest traps that can derail a leader's rhythm of consistency, is a thing called procrastination. Someone likened procrastination to credit card debt. It leads one to the mistaken belief that "Someday, some time, somehow...I will..."

We can even become professional procrastinators because the more we get good at it, the more comfortable we become with it and the more chances we take until it becomes a way of life. We should always do what needs to be done at any given point in time in a focussed and consistent manner. The saying goes - procrastination is the thief of time. What needs to be done today cannot unduly be postponed for tomorrow because tomorrow is never guaranteed. We need to maximise every day as a God – given opportunity. That is why it is called the present. What do you do with a present? You open it up and utilise it with an appreciation of its value. We also acknowledge the motive in which the gift has been made to you; it is an expression of the giver's intentions, devotion, and affection. Similarly, we cannot just disregard the opportunities granted to us and squander our time through procrastination.

We all have our fair share of pressure in life. Procrastination will never reduce or eliminate the pressure. We know exactly what to do but deliberately postpone and somehow refuse to do what we ought to do when it should be done. We know that a specific relationship is destructive, our spending does not match our income, some of our lifestyle habits are harmful to our health, busyness should never be at the expense of investing quality time with our family, the debilitating consequences of neglecting key spiritual disciplines like prayer and meditating on the Scriptures, bitterness and unforgiveness inhibits our capacity to engage in real and meaningful relationships; we know exactly what to do but choose to delay it. For some reason or the other, we postpone the obvious at our own peril.

Another aspect that exacerbates the habit of procrastination is when we are beset by many distractions. Linda Stone of Microsoft calls it the wired age, the age of continuous partial attention. There is a constant flood of emails, Facebook, Instagram, Twitter, and WhatsApp messages that is screaming for our attention. Then there are misplaced priorities that divert our focus, and our primary responsibilities are put on the back burner. In military terms, you need to establish "no fly zones" in your life. The military sometimes determines areas in which no civil aviation activities may take place. Any violation of that airspace would lead to an evacuation with sometimes fatal consequences. Likewise, we need to block out an hour or two in our day to work on the major priority for the day with no interference at all from cell phone calls or emails. Multi-tasking is not a virtue, focus increases productivity. Let us not allow the inbox to rule our lives.

Most of us do not take full responsibility to create for ourselves the future we want but are always waiting on someone to facilitate something on our behalf or being told by somebody else what they think is good for our lives. This approach to life robs us of our creativity, initiative, and self-actualization. It can also make us vulnerable to manipulation and exploitation. Possibility is your best friend; it follows you wherever you go. When we focus our attention on the right issues, it liberates us to create a new future. In order to transcend the realm of endless possibility, warrants that you and I deal with enemy number one, a thing called fear. It infiltrates our thoughts and our minds get pre-occupied with the fear of failure, rejection, inadequacy, what if and whatever.

The two most powerful yet contradictory emotions in life is fear and love. It is for this reason that 1 John 4: 18 (NKJV) declares "*There is no fear in love. But perfect love drives out all fear...the one who fears is not made perfect in love.*" Since our Creator is the Supreme source of love and always has our best interest at heart, we need to maintain a constant and interactive relationship with Him to negate the crippling effects of fear. Fear is an emotion and not necessarily a reality. More than 90% of the things we feared in life never materialised. It drains us emotionally, clouds our objectivity, suppresses our passion and diverts our energy into survival mode instead of venturing into the realm of endless possibility.

One of my biggest regrets in life is the inordinate amount of time wasted on delaying and postponing critical issues until it reached crisis proportions. In the process, I have not only lost precious time but have forfeited opportunities, delayed implementation of important goals in my life, risked my reputation, my self-esteem took a serious knock and I put myself under undue tension and anxiety. I made this sober discovery that there is such a thing as being too late.

May I invite you to seriously reflect on the following questions in addressing real or potential traits of procrastination in your life:

- Do I have a follow-through mindset? How will I rate my own effectiveness in following through to completion when embarking on an assignment?
- What kind of things occupy my time? Are they essential in my leadership role, bringing fulfilment and giving me the necessary reward for my effort?
- Do I fear change in my life, or will I rather maintain the status quo?
- Is failure fatal to me? Do I have such a perfectionist mindset whereby I will rather not risk anything in life out of fear that if I am not sure that it will be right the first time, I will rather not do it at all?
- What are the distractions in my life that diverts my attention from key priorities and in the process sacrificing truth for popularity?

May God grant us the appropriate discernment and grace to seize the moment with the necessary urgency and not get trapped in a state of perpetual procrastination. So much can go wrong through our inaction and so many people's lives can be adversely affected by it. It can result in a situation whereby your credibility might be liquidated. Tomorrow is today. Let us get going!

Our credibility hinges very heavily on our ability to maintain consistency in all our endeavours. When your name is mentioned, what should be foremost in people's minds is someone who is stable, reliable and dependable. And this should not be a once-off proposition but should be demonstrated regularly and consistently. Let consistency becomes the rhythm of the tune that we will dance to, in everything we do in life.

PITSTOP

In life we need to develop a rhythm within ourselves, our primary relationships, social activities, spirituality and just about everything. You cannot go about life in an erratic fashion. People should know where they stand with you. As indicated earlier, it is not what we do occasionally that will make us effective in life but what we do consistently. Let me share with you some of the rhythms which I built into my life :

1. I make the first cup of tea when we wake up in the morning for Liz and me, after going through the wake-up routine. We will then do our morning devotions by each reading and reflecting on our respective literature and related Bible reading. We will then exchange notes as to the application of what we have read on our personal, family, professional and social lives. After that we will then spend time in prayer. This rhythm sets the tone for our day.
2. As far as communication is concerned, we are forever talking about stuff, but we also built in the following rhythm to set aside dedicated time for meaningful engagement:
   - dialogue daily
   - date weekly
   - depart quarterly.

   Admittedly, the lockdown rules during Covid19 have disrupted our weekly and quarterly rhythms but we have applied this rhythm over many years now.
3. Family celebrations are critical. Birthdays, anniversaries, and special events should never be taken for granted. It does not always have to be a big bash but some structured form of activity to appreciate the journey traversed thus far and an expression of gratitude. Zoe's portfolio for many years now, has been to take care of the Christmas tree.
4. Church attendance is not optional, and my children knew this when they still lived with us. This rhythm is non-negotiable. We really miss church since the imposed lockdown due to the pandemic!
5. I check in with friends regularly. With the advent of Covid, this became even more critical. I cannot recall how many times I would get a call out of the blue from a friend and the timing would be perfect because at that moment I might be battling with something. That word of encouragement, listening ear or just

being there, has saved me from lapsing into a possible downward spiral.

6. Creating moments of solitude for myself. I used to go to a retreat centre in Hartbeespoort monthly just to unplug and spend time contemplating various issues. Unfortunately, the venue has since closed down because of the lockdown restrictions. I had to create some internal no-fly zones at home where I just find a quiet spot to reflect.
7. One cannot overemphasise the importance of going for a full scale annual medical check-up. Any potential problems can be detected early, and corrective action initiated timeously. This averted many possible health issues in my life. You must have a regular check-up or else you will checkout. I am in my mid - sixties and have been going through this routine for decades now.
8. When it comes to intimacy in marriage, can I take you into my confidence? The sexual act is just a culmination of all the signals, gestures and messages that were sent out throughout the day. It is not a matter of switching off the lights and merely pumping up the paraffin stove. No broer! If you want to have heaven at eleven, you must already start at seven. Let me repeat myself, heaven at eleven, starts at seven not five minutes before kick-off time. There should therefore be that conscious and deliberate yet tactical attempt to pursue each other right throughout the day.

The above is not an exhaustive list but just a few examples of some of the things I had to build into my daily, weekly, monthly, or annual routine consciously and deliberately. It brings about consistency in my life and by so doing, I was able to develop my credibility. The intense expectations from our daily lives can become a vicious cycle and cause burnout. This result in us being ineffective and simply lose our zeal and enthusiasm for our primary responsibilities. Building a rhythm into our lives, will greatly assists to keep us energised and move us forward in life.

The question that I would like to raise with you is "What makes you tick?" Passion is the fuel that drives behaviour and gives us a reason for being. Passion responds positively and decisively to things that make one glad, mad, or sad. For this to happen, we need to protect those things that compromise our passion by maintaining consistency in what we regard as vital in our lives. It is not a crime to say no. Whenever something encroaches on any area that maintains your rhythm in life, give it your urgent attention. Any delay in dealing with it and initiate the appropriate remedial action, can lead to dysfunctionality, or even become fatal in that area of your life.

Chapter 11

NURTURING A SPIRIT OF COMMUNITY

We are created as relational beings and we all have the need to experience community. That old saying - no man is an island, should not be taken lightly. We all want to be part of a group that has certain things in common with us and where we can give expression to our true identity. People with no credibility has a mindset of always getting as opposed to giving. On the other hand, those with credibility, reach out to others to create mutually enriching life experiences. The question I want to raise with you is: "When last have you done something for the first time in your life?" Become friends with people that are not your age group. Hang out with people whose first language is not the same as yours. Get to know someone that does not come from your social class. This is how you see the world. This is how you grow your world and broaden your circle of influence.

We are all human and we need to come to terms with the reality that there will not be any "perfect" life in any human form. None of us is the full package and this necessitates a sense of interdependency. Our modern lifestyles have regrettably distanced us from and somehow desensitised us to the harsh realities that some of our fellow human beings experience as a daily reality. It is also not just a matter of merely being aware of these realities, but continuously probing for appropriate responses to resolve or mitigate the situation for the better.

The foremost question that should always preoccupy our minds as we endeavour to change any given environment is: "What needs to change?" It might be that you need a change in the way you think. Perhaps you may have a deep-seated prejudice or favouritism. Maybe you need a change of words that might have reinforced negativity or discrimination and stereotyping but more importantly, you may need a change of your actions; uncompromisingly living out your values on being. This is crucial in enhancing your credibility.

Mastermind what the Master had in mind

We are all created equal by God in His image and likeness according to Genesis 1: 26. We should therefore live our lives reflective of this reality. In response to a question raised about what the most important commandments are, Jesus stated in Mark 12: 29 – 31 that firstly you should love the Lord your God with all your heart, soul, and mind and secondly, you should love your neighbour as yourself. God demands that we love everybody in our immediate sphere of influence regardless of class, creed, or colour and most importantly to love ourselves.

This was further amplified in the parable of the Good Samaritan. Historically the Jews did not want to have anything to do with the Samaritans. It was therefore a great shock to them when Jesus used the Samaritan, to exemplify what unconditional love and servanthood was all about. It was not the most politically correct thing to do but quite instructive about how God wants us to relate in a humane manner to people regardless of their background.

We started off very well in South Africa at the early stages of our new democratic dispensation in pursuit of Nelson Mandela's vision of a rainbow nation at peace with itself and the world. This work fizzled out as time went on because the work was not followed through with diligence until we finally have dealt with the demon of racism and any form of discrimination. The wise King Solomon puts it so succinctly in Song of Solomon 2: 15 (NIV) "*Catch for us the foxes, the little foxes that ruin the vineyards, our vineyards that are in bloom.*" Foxes represent all the hindrances, irritations and contradictions that distract us from our ability to bring about an absolutely free, equal and united nation focussed on creating a prosperous country. We have come a long way in building a new South Africa and some excellent things were accomplished in the life of our young nation. But some little foxes will always seek to spoil a growing fruitful vineyard. Likewise, we cannot leave the eradication of racism to chance indefinitely.

When incidents of blatant racism flare up in our country, we usually respond to it from a reactive stance and have not yet mastered the art of addressing it in an empowering manner. It is therefore incumbent on all South Africans and not only the political leadership, to urgently engage in the unfinished business of eliminating racism in all its shapes and forms. We need to get to grips as to how race as a body marker remains deeply entrenched in our social psyche and performs the function of dividing humans. In the process, it has robbed us of the opportunity to co-exist in harmony as equals.

What can you and I do in our individual capacities to meaningfully contribute towards this important work?

- Guard against stereotyping and generalizations. I like what Chimanda Adichie says about it *"The problem with stereotypes is not that they are untrue, but they are incomplete. They make one story become the only story."*[54] Every human being has a story to be validated. No matter who you are, how experienced you are and how knowledgeable you think you are, always delay judgement. How many times in your life and mine were we proven to be wrong regarding opinions formed about people or groups, without knowing all the facts?
- Be vigilant about unconscious bias. Bias is a prejudice in favour of or against one thing, person or a group compared with another usually in a way considered to be unfair. We can sometimes so easily just act out of habit without even thinking about how it affects those around us. Always seek to honestly interrogate your own motives and actions in terms of exclusion, sensitivity, and respect.

- Create opportunities to engage in open discussion about the realities of racism in your sphere of influence. In one of the very large services companies I am involved with, I was so encouraged by the CEO personally leading Diversity Beyond the Numbers Workshops throughout the various regions. It is crucial to hold honest conversations about the "taken-for-granted" internalised superiority and internalised inferiority produced by decades of racial segregation.
- As parents we need to model the right values in our families. No child is born a racist. The family is the primary arena for socialization. If we constantly express our prejudice and racist notions to our children, it will negatively shape their outlook towards life and their ability to engage appropriately with the outside world.
- Speak the truth in love. It is not always what we say but how we say it. Most of the time we do not talk about racism in a rational and objective manner but rather from a position of frustration and protest.
- Do not live your life to get even but to move ahead. When the issue of racism comes up, we are conveniently told not to rehash the past. The past should however not only be used to seek retribution but however uncomfortable it might sound, must assist us as a reference point in shaping the desired future.

I interact quite extensively with a wide range of people in our country across the class, religious and racial spectrum on a frequent basis. By all indications there is a tremendous amount of goodwill and ordinary people are doing extraordinary things to improve the lot of their fellow countrymen. During the peak of the Covid-19 pandemic, I was instilled with such a great deal of pride and hope when I saw the level of generosity demonstrated by people from all walks of life in a manner never seen in my lifetime in our country. We owe it not only to ourselves but also to future generations to co-create the desired inclusive and prosperous society characterised by respect for our common humanity and affirmation of our rich diversity.

Let us unite and go for those foxes!

Leave the seat and join the circle

Building community is deliberate and intentional. Most people go about their lives as if they sit in the seat of an auditorium in a row where they can have the best view of the stage. Since they have paid for their seat, there is an expectation of getting value for money from the performance. Sitting in that seat warrants no effort from their side; everything is left in the capable hands of the director, conductor, keynote speaker, headline act or whatever form of performance they came to watch. At the end of the show, they can express a legitimate critique of the outcome without even having a clue of what it took to bring the production or performance into being.

How many times have we sat in the company of people who often ascribe to themselves a right to pass judgement on the noble efforts of others from a position of passivity. You will frequently hear them saying that things are out of control because of the government, their pastor, boss, the capitalists, the unions, the young people, the White people, the Black people, the foreigners.... and the list continues.

On the other hand, there is a silent majority who have taken the responsibility to move out of their seats and made themselves available to operate in a circle of authentic relationships and community. Instead of just facing the stage, they face each other and join hands in unison towards a common purpose. The circle is symbolic of a collaborative effort and an expression of inter – dependency. Each one realises that together they can accomplish more as they tap into the collective wisdom of each other. The circle sets boundaries for acceptable conduct and accountability, engenders community, fosters relational integrity and disarms us from any form of pretence. Yes, there might be legitimate reasons to raise concerns and dissent for what is going wrong in our society, but they are solution-seekers. In the final analysis, they respond to challenges to turn things around for the better, mindful of the fact that destiny is in their own hands. It is the ability to reach out into the unknown, yet with a firm resolve on possibilities. This is the space where their credibility is progressively shaped.

Obsession with self is increasingly becoming the norm of our day and age. This leads to a situation where people are so quick to deflect attention from themselves and pass key responsibilities on to others. Their favourite response is: "It's them!" If everything revolves around us, then we are prone to act out of character and not being truthful to ourselves. The world is yearning for authenticity; real people in a real world, confronting the real issues of the day in a real and collaborative manner.

Those operating in a circle, are focused on building community. Their pursuit is not based on selfish ideals but their outlook on life is holistic. Their foremost concern is what kind of world they will leave behind than the one they are currently living in. They see the world from a legacy perspective. In the words of Brene Brown *"Belonging is the innate human desire to be part of something larger than us. True belonging only happens when we present our authentic, imperfect selves to the world."* [55]

Never in the history of mankind have we experienced such levels of connectivity through all the various technological advancements, yet from a relational point of view, humanity is at its worst point of disconnectedness. I will be the first to admit that getting connected is not always that easy. Rick Warren in one of his recent articles suggests that there are three fears that we all must fight against. There is the fear that we will be exposed for who we really are. Secondly, there is the fear of being rejected. Lastly, the fear that we will be hurt again.[56]

The following are some key pointers in working through these fears and fostering meaningful connectedness:

- Accept yourself and have a healthy regard for your own uniqueness. Never underestimate the contribution you can make no humble it might be, for a just cause in your own name and right.
- Always evaluate your motives, doing the right things for the right reasons.
- Maintain an open and responsive attitude. Allow the insights and perspectives of others to help shape your thinking and never assume yourself to be better than others.
- Do not be defensive but readily own up for mistakes when they occur. If you chop wood, there is bound to be splinters. There are people who are so obsessed with protecting their reputation that

any form of failure resembles a train smash. Saying "I was wrong", is the hallmark of maturity.

- Love, love and love some more. The love of others and their well-being, should be our primary motivation. Andrew Hess said, *"The true test of love is when they offend you or you offend them, you move towards them instead of moving away from them."* [57]

We are facing daunting socio-economic challenges in our country. This will require from all of us to get out of our seats of comfort and convenience and join hands with others in a circle of authentic relationships. Is the well-being of the society in which you operate, still uppermost on your mind or is it only about your own interest? What are your fears? Are you prepared to take the risk and make yourself known for who you really are? Credibility is shaped in community. If we tap into our collective ingenuity, we can make a difference in our society and contribute towards a better world.

The forgotten virtue of kindness

There is a type of misplaced assertiveness operative in society that can at times be rather blunt and brutal. The word kindness sounds like such a weak concept, yet it is one of the most powerful forces that fosters meaningful community. Kindness is not only about being nice, generous, and polite; it is revolutionary. Never underestimate how a small gesture of kindness can radically change the life of someone forever. It might be a kind word, a hand of assistance, a complimentary remark for a job well done, connecting someone to access information that will enable the individual to progress in life, a hug, a reaffirming handshake, writing that small note of encouragement, buying that small gift of appreciation…. yet expressing it in a sincere and gracious manner.

There are many lonely, depressed, hurting, rejected and unloved people out there. They might appear alright but may be grappling with a lot of issues on the inside. Kindness in its simplest form even if it is just a smile, can bring warmth to a cold heart and lonely existence. We must therefore cultivate a keen sensitivity and be kind, for everyone you meet is fighting a battle you know nothing about. John Bunyan puts it so beautifully *"You have not lived today until you have done something for someone that can never repay you."* [58]

Whatever we do, it should never be about ourselves but viewed as a unique opportunity as being an extension of God's love to humanity. If we recognise and affirm the goodness in others through the sweetness of our generosity, they will start appreciating not only the goodness in us but also the goodness in themselves. It is always so reassuring when you discover that others believe in you. I am sure it will elevate your mood to know that there are still some good people out there and not allow one or a few not too pleasant incidences, cause you to give up hope on your current reality.

I have been blessed by the generosity of countless people that altered the destiny of my life. The best I can do now, is to continue imparting kindness and generosity into the lives of those in my immediate sphere of influence. There were teachers and community members who helped me during my schooling days when my mom single handed kept the home fires burning under very impoverished circumstances. In my professional career I had mentors who unselfishly invested their time and expertise to prepare me for my future leadership assignments. I have a close circle of friends, whose companionship, mutual accountability, prayers, and support has carried me over many years now. I have fellow believers who for decades now, have journeyed with me to seek after God with me. I have a beautiful wife and family who love and respect me so abundantly; where kindness, generosity and mutual respect have become the hallmark of our interaction with one another. My life in essence is the sum total of all the kind inputs, unselfish commitment and unconditional love that I have been blessed with from ordinary men and woman from diverse backgrounds in society.

We are all creatures of habit. The experts suggest that it takes 21 days to create a habit. May I challenge you that over the next 21 days to commit and diligently practice the following:

1. The words that will come out of my mouth, will only be to build others up without any hint of malicious intent.

2. Every day I will actively seek new ways of extending kindness to others.
3. I will be kind and gentle to myself; appreciating who I am and take good care of myself. Being kind towards yourself can sometimes be the hardest thing to do.
4. I will make a special attempt to see the good in others, expressing it personally if possible, to them and becoming less critical of their faults and shortcomings.

I can assure you that by just refocussing on the four aspects above, will bring a total paradigm shift in your approach to life. It will not only engender higher levels of fulfilment but even more importantly, change the lives of others for the better. In a world that is sometimes reckless, heartless, and thoughtless, we should become the embodiment of His loving kindness. It might seem insignificant to you, but kindness is one of the biggest contributions you can make to humanity.

Immigration – a new reality of our times

According to the United Nation Department of Economic and Social Affairs Report, international migrants reached an estimated 272 million people by the end of 2019. It represents an increase of 51 million since 2010. Currently, international migrants represent 3,5% of the global population.[59] Immigration has major impacts on both the people and places involved in it.

Closer home, immigration has also become a hot topical issue in South Africa. It is still anybody's guess how many immigrants actually live in South Africa. Official figures suggest 3 million, but some unofficial reports estimate that the undocumented portion can put this number as high as 4,5 million. Since the advent of our new democratic dispensation, South Africa has been viewed by many as the El Dorado of the continent, attracting many economic immigrants and asylum seekers. With a very shaky economic situation currently in our country, the competition for scarce resources and opportunities are becoming fierce and sometimes volatile.

Immigration has both a positive and negative side to a country's socio-economic well-being.

On the positive side:

- It can augment the skills deficit of the host country especially in areas where rapid growth is imminent for economic development.
- Immigrants can bring innovation, new levels of energy and international best practice.
- The host country can be enriched through a culturally diverse experience.
- Over time, the country of origin might benefit from savings accumulated, skills acquired, and international networks established.

On the negative side:

- Immigrant workers can be exploited, leading to depressed wage levels.
- Unexpected population increases can put a burden on the delivery of public services.
- Ease of movement by undocumented immigrants, can attract unscrupulous characters that may trigger criminal activities and necessitate greater deployment of security capability.
- Family instability whereby children may grow up without parental input.

Jesus was also an immigrant at some stage of His life. It is recorded in Mathew 2 how Joseph and Mary had to flee to Egypt with Jesus when He was still a little child. Herod was busy with a serious campaign of genocide of any boy child from Jewish decent. During Christ's crucifixion, it was also an immigrant called Simon from Cyrene (current Libya on the African continent) who was forced by the Roman soldiers to help Him carry the cross when He agonized under the pain and suffering. Joseph, Moses, Daniel, and Esther are but few notable examples that served as foreigners not by choice, in great kingdoms yet mightily used by God, to change the destiny of the nation.

"And He has made from one blood every nation of men to dwell on all the face of the earth and has determined their pre-appointed times and the boundaries of their dwellings." Acts 17:26 (NKJV) We should therefore be well advised never to look down on other people just because they come from a different country. Leviticus 19:33-34 (AMP) further emphasize this point *"When a stranger resides with you in your land, you shall not oppress or mistreat him. But the stranger who resides with you shall be to you as one of the same country and you shall love him as yourself...."*

I cannot even contemplate what is going on in the hearts and minds of those who daily get uprooted from their place of origin due to external circumstances like war, famine, political instability and other natural disasters totally beyond their control. The Biblical injunction around immigrants, compels us to build community with them as one of our primary responsibilities in being human. Just some practical suggestions to assist in this regard:

1. You might know someone in your company, church or community from a foreign country that might do with a bit of help. Reach out to them and get familiar with the facts to be an extension of God's love towards them.
2. Expose your children to continuous interaction with people of other cultures or circumstances. It prepares them to be open and comfortable with people anywhere they might find themselves in this world. Isolation heightens the fear of the unknown.
3. Pray for those that are on the forefront of missionary or relief agency work for strength, protection, and wisdom. Also pray for those that are involved in immigration policy formulation for a balance of the rule of law and humane compassion.
4. Adopt a charitable cause that ameliorates the plight of refugees or people in distress in a foreign country. Seek God's guidance on what sacrifices you must make and what you can commit to.
5. Respect the God given dignity of every person. Refrain from any misguided thoughts, words, and actions. Generalizations can be foolhardy and dangerous.

The inequality gap globally, remains the elephant in the room and is simply unsustainable. Unless there is radical action in this regard, this vicious cycle of forced immigration can have a serious destabilizing effect on the world. Whilst the pressing reality of immigration cannot be discounted, we should never behave like Cain by asking this very dismissive question: "Am I my brother's keeper?"

Will the next generation know?

The community of faith is one of the most important anchors of society. We are charged with building that community diligently right from the family foundation. This has inter- generational implications.

Israel entered the Promised Land under Joshua's leadership and at the age of 110 years he died. His contemporaries also died over a period of time, having witnessed all the great things God had done for the nation in their lifetime and they prospered in their new environment. However, in Judges 2:10 (NKJV) we are made aware of a very disturbing trend "... *another generation arose after them who did not know the Lord nor the work which He had done for Israel.*" They forsook the Lord and got themselves involved in idolatry, arousing God's anger.

If we are not vigilant as a country, a similar set of circumstances might play itself out in the near future. God has miraculously led us through a bloodless changeover of authority from the demonic system of apartheid into our current democratic dispensation. Two important lessons are of extreme relevance for our future sustainability as a country. Firstly, when the knowledge of God is preserved in a community by those who experienced His power in their past lives, righteousness increases, and the people prosper. Secondly, parents have a responsibility not to allow their children to grow up without the knowledge of God. Living in ignorance and disconnected from their Creator will result in them going after false gods. This will not only lead to self-destruction but the demise of future generations.

If you visit our churches on a Sunday, in most instances the congregation is made up of elderly people and in very rare circumstances will you find an overwhelmingly young audience in attendance. Are we veering towards a situation of a generation that neither knows the Lord nor what He has done for our country?

There are many great luminaries of the faith from our country such as Chief Albert Luthuli, Beyers Naude, Desmond Tutu, Frank Chikane, Peter Storey to name but a few, as well as countless ordinary men and women whose faith carried us through the dark days of our past. They persevered amidst trying circumstances for us to have reached our promised land. It is our responsibility to continuously remind the younger generation of our rich spiritual heritage and keep them connected to their faith, lest they wander away and put the country on a slippery slope.

It is therefore our responsibility not to only remind the younger generation about our spiritual heritage but through fostering proper relationships with them. This will go a long way to build a community of young people who will know their God. As they grow up in this community, it will assist in building a healthy pipeline of leadership for generations to come. Let us never forget where we come from. To preserve our proud spiritual heritage, we will be well advised to make God the centre of all our endeavours.

I would like to address myself specifically to fathers as the head of your home. Be the king, priest, and prophet of your home in a serious and diligent manner. Our children are going to discover for themselves about the world around them and their specific role in it. If they do not learn it from us, they are going in any way learn it from other people. The latter might not necessarily be informed by the right values. It is therefore of paramount importance that we model appropriate Christian values to them. We also have a responsibility to teach our children what matters to God. There is no greater responsibility we can have in life than reflecting God's image for our children to see. They should be able to observe in us real faith informed by loving God and loving others.

God uses people to help people. To most of us, this is unknown territory. Life is about risk taking, taking well calculated risks. It is about honest engagement and building up a relationship of trust. Trust pushes you into another dimension, from a place of relative safety to a position of making yourself vulnerable. It can at times bring some discomfort but can lead to immeasurable opportunities and fulfilment as you learn new things about yourself and others. At times you might even have to unlearn unsubstantiated and downright archaic views you held about other people as you pursue authentic and meaningful community.

PITSTOP

I am a relational person and thrive on community. Life favoured my family and I with such a rare opportunity as the seeds were sown at the very nascent stages of our family life, to prepare us to function in a new society that did not even existed by then. To illustrate this point - I worked in Tshepong Hospital that catered primarily for Black African patients, I stayed in a Coloured area, my children attended a predominantly Indian school because I wanted them to have an English medium of instruction. On Sundays we worshipped at Rhema Church which by then was predominantly White and to crown it all, I married a Motswana girl! Oh yes, I paid lobola and I am the eldest mokgwenyane (son-in-law). Very few people at that time of enforced racial division and the apartheid architecture, had such a privilege to comfortably transition from one group to the other all in one day. It was therefore not such a big deal to hand over my eldest daughter in marriage in 2012 to the Harrison family in Australia.

When I went into deeper engagements with people from all these different backgrounds, I discovered for myself that we had so much more in common than the things that were artificially dividing us. It brought me to the realisation that I should never get ensnared in generalisations and racial stereotyping. The danger in this, is that you want to make your story the only story to the exclusion of other people's experiences. I also realised how important it is for me as the head of my home to inculcate in the hearts of my children, the principle of respect for others regardless of race, colour, or creed. This set of circumstances spurred me on to work relentlessly for social justice towards the normalisation of our society.

We are living in an age of modernity where the relevance of cultural heritage is in many respects questioned and not as pronounced as in previous generations. What can however not be argued against, is that culture gives us a sense of identity and belonging, whereby we feel connected to those espousing the same values, beliefs, and customs. There is a richness in African culture that greatly influenced my outlook on life. Liz and I come from different cultural backgrounds. This necessitated that I should develop a clear understanding on matters that were culturally significant. Some of my most culturally enriching experiences include - being invited for the first time by the elders to be part of lobola negotiations, the intricacies of managing family politics and protocols during funeral arrangements, sitting around the fire in a rural village during quite a few night vigils listening to the wisdom and historical anecdotes of the older men and just observing the elevated respect bo malome (uncles) enjoy in the family hierarchy. With simplicity and an unsophisticated approach to life, their presence speaks of authority, wisdom and custodianship of the values, customs and practices in their families and community at large.

In church circles, I also had the privilege over many years now, to minister across the racial divide both in all the major urban centres as well as in some of the most rural settings in our country and on the African continent. Leadership development is one of my biggest passions. God also favoured me with many opportunities where I have helped churches especially from disadvantaged areas in envisioning processes, strengthening of governance and just being a trusted coach and mentor to some in the leadership echelons. It is my insight into the cultural nuances built up over many years of interaction with different racial groups, that enhanced my effectiveness in this regard.

Allow me to share a few observations (let me hasten to emphasise that these are mere observations) that I experienced in the church world and please hold back your rocks for now:

- When it comes to punctuality, White churches are very strict in this regard whereas in Black churches it sometimes takes a bit of time to get started but once they get going, it's difficult to stop. By being too rigid on time where people look at their watches constantly should church go over the scheduled time, can suppress spontaneity in our worship. On the other hand, we should not allow ill-discipline by not being punctual or drag things on without any purpose. So, we need to take the strengths of both sides and it will result into a unique South African experience.

- Some White congregants really struggle to sing without musical accompaniment whereas Black congregations are comfortable singing a-carpella without accompaniment, with a great variation of melody and improvisation. Worship takes on a very expressive and spontaneous form in Black Churches and dancing comes naturally whereas the established churches are a bit more laid back.
- In Black Pentecostal and Charismatic circles, the service can be quite loud with regular punctuation of Amens and Hallelujahs which makes ministry quite a vibey experience. Whereas in White churches the audience is more subdued.
- The rhythm in the way we clap hands… let's rather not go there.

Is there anything wrong with any of our different approaches? Not at all. This is a function of socialization and just the way we are wired. Cross-cultural pollination will enrich our own experiences, help us to have an appreciation for our uniqueness and strengthen unity of purpose in our diversity. It will also disarm us from our own ignorance and pride. The latter manifests itself in the following ways: pride of face, pride of race and pride of grace. I do not need to remind you about how God despises the proud. In fostering community in His church, this element should not be found amongst us. What is important is that our hearts are all in the right place, a love for God and a love for people.

The Lord has really graced me to operate at a transcultural level with relative ease. Even my unpleasant experiences with some conservative Afrikaners during our unfortunate past, did not cause bitterness in my life. As a matter of fact, some of my most trusted friends come from the Afrikaner community as being the case in all other racial groups. Between 2009 – 2012, I was in the leadership of the Afrikaanse Handels Instituut – by then one of the biggest organised business chambers in South Africa. I was elected President of the organisation in 2011. We fostered great partnerships between business, government, and civil society by tapping into some of the expertise and resourcefulness of Afrikaner businessmen in places like Harrismith, Bela Bela, Phillipolis, Modimolla, Kou-Kamma, Saldanha, Potchefstroom to name but a few. We were able to make tangible interventions that uplifted communities and made valuable policy inputs on local economic development.

South Africa's biggest asset is the quality of its people. People with the resilience to succeed with a never-say-die kind of attitude.

David Murray once said, "*There is a characteristic that separates the successful from the unsuccessful in every walk of life – teachability.*" [60] A teachable person does not just talk all the time but is one who has learned the art of listening with purpose in pursuit of mutual learning. A teachable person also handles criticism and correction appropriately without resentment or retaliation. Much of our problems can be ascribed to an unwillingness to learn from the real-life experiences of others. In pursuit of building community, I thank God for the many learning opportunities granted to me; it really positioned me and my family to make a humble contribution towards a better South Africa.

PART C – A CALL TOWARDS CHANGE

Chapter 12

YOU MAKE YOUR DECISIONS AND YOUR DECISIONS MAKE YOU

You know exactly where you stand with leaders who have credibility because they take responsibility for all their actions and the consequences of their decisions. They are the first to own up for their mistakes and make a concerted effort to initiate corrective action to prevent a similar set of circumstances. You might not always get it perfectly right the first time because there might have been unforeseen and unavoidable variables that you did not factor in as you embarked on your journey. However, it is the ability to reflect, make the necessary adjustments and move forward, that will enhance your credibility. The journey is more important than the destination. The question is "How hungry are you for it?"

I recently tuned into one of the radio talk shows while on the road. Callers were asked by the talk show host to share some of their biggest regrets they had in their lives. Some shared why they regretted having married at such a young age with little experience about life, not having taken their education seriously and were now struggling. Others regretted making a wrong career move. Some called in and recalled taking the first drink during varsity days which progressively veered into a level where drinking had become an obsession, years down the line. Others regretted having neglected their health and were now suffering from preventable lifestyle diseases. There were also strong relational regrets about how a casual fling progressively destroyed a happy marriage. One person mentioned the emotional abuse and manipulation of a close friend that she trusted. These accounts are indeed very thought provoking.

We all have our own catalogue of regrets regarding poor decisions we made that had long-lasting implications. When asked for a reason, some can easily make light of it by saying "I was simply just too angry", "too proud", "so lonely and very desperate", or simply "not really thinking about it" But in the quietness of our thoughts, regrets can persistently haunt us. As I listened to the radio, I also jogged my memory and recalled some decisions I had made in life. Upon reflection, there are quite a few that I am definitely not proud of at all, which had adverse consequences on my life.

For this input, I will confine myself to some of my leadership decisions that caused very intense regrets. Let me also state upfront that all these experiences also created opportunities for me to learn good from things that go bad. I can summarize some of my major leadership regrets as follows:

1. Trusting too easily: I am naturally a very relational person and usually look for the positive side in people. At times I just trusted too easily and never gave myself sufficient time to do a proper due diligence on an individual before bringing him or her into my leadership circle. I recall the consequences when I appointed a Marketing Executive based on a strong recommendation from one of my close associates, when I was CEO at SABS. The individual used to work in one of the leading financial companies in our country. Within five months of working for me, he abused the company credit card and promptly resigned when confronted, before I could initiate disciplinary processes. I later discovered that he was also involved in some form of financial impropriety, at his previous workplace. Because of this episode, there was a bit of a credibility deficit between me and my executive team in relation to my sense of judgement and it took me a bit of time to eliminate the deficit.

When I exited politics, I was approached by a gentleman who interacted with me quite frequently in political circles, to become one of the Black Economic Empowerment partners in a very lucrative meat processing business. At the time when all the shareholders went to sign the final papers at the bank for a loan of R18 million, my partner was conveniently sick and not available. He rocked up two days after that at the bank and I was pleasantly surprised to later discover that he never signed but it was his mother who actually signed. About a year into this deal, one of my close friends confronted me about this business relationship and expressed his disappointment about me not having done a proper due diligence on the said individual. It then came to light that my partner was sequestrated two years before we signed the deal, and he therefore did not legally qualify to enter into any financial contracts. He basically leveraged from my good name and reputation with financial institutions to secure the deal. Suffice to say, this relationship did not last because my partner became very disruptive in the business operations. The other shareholders voted for his exit. Fortunately, the business experienced excellent growth after his exit and we were able to pay off our liabilities to the bank. However, the scars of this toxic relationship remain.

2. Putting your life on hold to advance the agenda of someone else: On too many occasions, out of a genuine desire not to disappoint people I trusted, I was drawn into very intensive assignments that had no relationship to the immediate objectives I had set for my own life. My day was filled with meetings, travel, and functions without accomplishing anything of substance. The lure of being associated with something bigger, more exciting, and even influential names attached to it, has at times put my life on pause and also led me into unnecessary detours. I regretted the times when I was basically paraded as a trophy to validate the agendas of others with nothing of value to show. Determine your own agenda in life or others will do it on your behalf.

3. Underestimating corporate culture: I thrive on performance and results. There were instances where I experienced enormous frustration and resistance in organisations in which I led transformation initiatives. It was not because of the wrong strategy but because I discounted the values, practices and traditions embedded in the organisation.

One area where my skills set was indeed tested in this regard was the nine years that I was Chairperson of the Mineworkers Provident Fund. The mining industry is highly unionised and at times a very militant environment. Half of the Board of 18 trustees consisted of representatives of the unions and the other half out of employee representatives. Only the Chairperson of the Audit and Risk Committee and myself, were independent trustees. The slow pace at which decisions were arrived at during Board meetings, used to initially frustrate me a lot. Unions thrive on a consultative culture, and they will not move forward with a major decision, without seeking a mandate from their membership. Things became trickier when the dominance of the National Union of Mineworkers (NUM) which was a founding sponsor of the Fund, was challenged by a rival union called the Association of Mineworkers and Construction Union (AMCU). Because the rules of the Fund prescribe proportional representation, AMCU was allocated four seats on the Board, which did not go down well with the NUM. The rivalry between these two groupings had a negative spill over effect in the manner which discussions took place and how we ultimately arrived at decisions.

I had to learn to respect the way they engaged on issues and perspectives different from my own, through honest engagement. People will accept change if their views are respected and been given a chance to express it openly and honestly until progressively persuaded into a more superior alternative of doing things. Always build on the good that exists.

4. Perfectionism: Since my head was on the block as the leader, I would sometimes take work out of people's hands if there was any doubt that they would not perform to expectations. I was very impatient, and this led to undue pressure, conflict and even burn - out. Mastering the art of delegation and even allowing room for mistakes towards learning and development, rescued me from this destructive tendency. By this I am not in any way compromising on excellence but an honest recognition that perfection is a process.

I will always have respect for a gentleman called Phineas Tjie, my former Head of Department (HOD) whilst being MEC of Finance. He had a very unassuming personality, personified utmost integrity, and knew exactly how to marshal his troops to get the job done. At times when I veered into my perfectionist streak, he had this characteristic stutter to tell me tactfully *"MEC please get out of the way and let me and my team deal with the matter!"* Fortunately, I have come a long way in this regard and have learned the art of empowerment and deployment with authority.

5. Neglecting primary relationships: At the early stages of my leadership journey, everything revolved around me, my and I. Being so pre - occupied about making a name for myself, came at great expense to my family. When I realised this, my son and eldest daughter were already teenagers and there were just so many milestones in their lives which I had not been a part of. I merely got executive summaries from my wife about what was happening in their lives. Through God's grace I worked very hard to get balance back into my life and can honestly say that family relationships rank amongst the top priorities in my life.

What are the decisions that you have taken in your life that triggered perpetual regrets? Life is just too short to wake up every morning with regrets. We will have to deal with it appropriately by analyzing the root cause, learn from our mistakes, let go and genuinely commit to the best possible alternatives. If left unattended, it can cause serious damage and negatively frame your outlook towards life. Regrets can make you bitter, riddled with guilt and distract you from your mission in life. It can put you in a mind-set where you want to make up for lost ground and unduly overextend yourself even to a point of total disillusionment.

In Psalm 90: 12 (NIV) David reminds us *"Teach us to number our days, that we may gain a heart of wisdom."* Wisdom is the art of living well. There is absolutely no value in trying to defend or undo what has been done. Walking in wisdom also implies that if given a similar set of circumstances, what will I do differently. May God grant you His wisdom and grace to make wise decisions.

For everything there is a season

I am quite often approached by people who are confronted with a difficult decision and need advice about whether they should stay or exit their current situation. This ranges from changing employment, terminating a business partnership, resigning from a specific leadership position, severing ties in a long-standing friendship, whether they should stay on in a town or relocate to another one and the most difficult one is when someone is at the crossroads about continuing with a marriage relationship. People want to leave a specific environment for various reasons. Some of the reasons are borne out of a progressive build-up of frustrations due to unmet expectations, emotional abuse, a toxic environment, betrayal, or sometimes just plain boredom. In a marriage relationship when divorce papers are served, lawyers have conveniently coined a rationale called irreconcilable differences.

Leaving can at times be impulsive and people abandon an environment very easily without calculating the implications. We live in a generation of quitters where people are not prepared to go the extra mile, and grow in commitment. People can also launch themselves prematurely into positions for which they are ill prepared, seduced by the lure of money and status. Notwithstanding the feeling of being unappreciated, devalued and not optimally utilized, we should be careful not to indiscriminately throw in the towel and jump ship at the drop of a hat. By staying, persevering, and hanging on when quitting seems like the obvious option, creates an invaluable learning opportunity to build character, endurance and earns us the respect and influence of our peers.

There are however situations where it is necessary for you to exit not just for the sake of leaving but based on sound considerations that are intuitive, not taken under duress, but has developed over a period; is visionary and for the common good. It may even be disruptive to your comfort zone because you are stretched and challenged as you enter unchartered waters. One of my mentors advised me that I should never overstay my brief in any leadership position. I should always treat my environment as rented space and not think that I had the title deed on it.

All great leaders have a sense of discernment to know the right time for them to depart from the stage in an orderly fashion. People should not ask whether you were pushed or did you jump. Leadership on our continent of Africa labors under a very regressive phenomenon where leaders hang onto power for dear life, becoming obstacles towards progress. Arguably the best example ever set was by one of the world's greatest statesman,

Nelson Mandela. To voluntary resign after just one term in office, is indeed a shining example of a leader who had the requisite discernment of knowing when to go.

At some stage of my life, I had a very successful two terms as the first MEC of Finance in the North West Province. It was quite an agonizing experience to decide whether I should leave or stay on for another term at the peak of my tenure. I spent a week with my wife in a resort in Limpopo where we had very intense conversations about the future, spent quite a bit of time in prayer and meditation on the Word and later on also sought wise counsel from some of my close confidants. Once it was confirmed in our hearts that it was time to move on, I trusted God for the courage to follow through on the decision. At that time, I did not even know where I am going to be employed, but the Lord led me out of my comfort zone and all the potential trappings of political power into a challenging yet life-changing environment of the corporate world. If I overstayed my brief in politics, I would have sadly missed out on all the wonderful learning opportunities I went through both locally and internationally in the many influential positions I was blessed with in the corporate space. It takes courage to let go and explore new territories. Be sensitive and have a sense of discernment because God can sometimes open a door for what is next, when you least expected it. A few years ago, I had to transition again from formal executive employment to being self-employed. What lessons have I learned during these transitions?

1. Always check your passion barometer: When you wake up in the morning, you should go and do the things you want to do and not merely the things you have to do. Sometimes it has got absolutely nothing to do with the environment in which you currently operate but when the passion is not at peak levels, it might just be an indication that it is time to move on.
2. Never fall into the trap of being in maintenance mode: One can so easily lapse into a comfort zone once you have mastered a specific environment. Sometimes it needs a different person with a different skill-set to take the organisation to another level and you need to have the maturity to exit voluntarily. Your continued presence might be acceptable to maintain the status quo but

you are depriving the organisation of unlocking its maximum potential by holding on. Always reinvent yourself and seek new opportunities for personal growth.

3. Alignment with the vision: Never stay on in an environment where the organisational vision is not in alignment with your own vision and values in life. A lot of energy might unnecessarily be spent in contestation which is not fair on the organisation or healthy for your own well-being. As a matter of fact, issues of vision and values should have been clarified long before you enrolled for the assignment. Do not under-estimate corporate culture and think you can fix it once you are on the inside.
4. Never become a prisoner of a pay cheque: Yes, we all want a fair reward for our toil and sweat but money should never be the major motivator for you to stay on in a specific environment.
5. Do not be rushed into a decision: Qualitative decisions are based on qualitative information. Work through the tensions, questions, and uncertainties until there is clarity of direction. Once a decision has been taken, you must live with its consequences.
6. Be cognisant of your calling: Making the transition from formal employment to self-employment, was largely informed by a desire to optimally live out my calling of developing Christian leaders in the marketplace for Kingdom impact. To do that, I needed a greater margin of time and flexibility to enhance my scope and influence in this regard.

Are you by any chance in the valley of decision making? Is there a degree of anxiety that calls for an appropriate response? Is there a desire for something different than the status quo? My friend, I was there before. Do not become irrational in your decision making. Constantly ask God for the wisdom to discern when to engage and when to retreat, when to speak and when to keep quiet, when to stay and when to move on.

Missed opportunities can be costly

I do not know about you, but in my own life I can recall many opportunities that I allowed to pass by and regrettably those choices costed me dearly. I would have been in much better shape if I invested more time in my education when the scholarship was up for the taking, not being too overly risk averse when some very good business deals came my way, being more available to my children when they were still young; now the nest is empty, being more disciplined in my saving habits, investing more time in nurturing solid friendships……. quite a list.

Nothing great ever happens without an element of risk. Life is about taking risks, well calculated risks. We all agree that someone needs to take the first step but normally respond by saying as long as it is not me. In the process we do not live to our true purpose. Each one of us has been given a unique assignment or purpose in life. Unless you have a clear understanding of why you are here, then you are going to lose out on many life defining opportunities. Allow me to just highlight some of the reasons in my observation, why we lose out on opportunities:

1. Laziness: Nothing will just fall into your lap; every opportunity needs to be activated through diligent effort. Sometimes it might necessitate a season of preparation and sowing the appropriate seeds in anticipation of a harvest. This requires work. There is only one place where success appears before work and that is in the Oxford Dictionary.
2. Fear: The paralysing effect of the fear of possible failure, can cloud one's objectivity towards new possibilities. Failure and setbacks have the potential to create tremendous opportunities for growth in critical areas like perseverance, patience and character.
3. Familiarity: Some people in our existing circles as precious as they might be, can become predictable in their responses. I call them the beige brigade. This can have the adverse effect of holding us back in pursuit of our dreams because they might merely not have anything new to offer to assist us in moving forward. By this I

do not mean that you should undermine people in your existing circles. They might have been there like the primary school teacher to get you through the basics but certainly not equipped to assist you becoming a rocket scientist.

4. Exaggerated expectations: Most of us are always on the lookout for the great and spectacular stuff. In the process we lose out on the small things that holds great potential for positioning us into a niche space. Great opportunities are always disguised in small packages. Sometimes the little things in life are steppingstones to the big opportunities. Have a sense of awareness not to lose out on these opportunities.

Through God's grace I was able to successfully navigate through quite a lot of obstacles in my life. Mistakes, oh yes, they were numerous. Lost opportunities; honestly quite a number. But on the occasions where I seized the moment, my life has irrevocably been transformed and my potential has been stretched. Leonard Ravenhill said, *"An opportunity of a lifetime must be seized in the lifetime of the opportunity."* [61] My biggest challenge moving forward, is to live my life in such a way that one day when I slow down on my normal routine and exit from my current portfolio of leadership responsibilities, I will be tormented by this perennial question – Why did I not seize that opportunity?

David's words in Psalm 90: 12 (PT) is quite instructive in this regard " *Help us to remember that our days are numbered and help us to interpret our lives correctly. Set your wisdom deeply in our hearts....*"

The power of surrender

I am a very organised person who believes in processes, rigorous execution of plans and meeting envisaged deadlines. These are extremely essential things that we need to factor into all our endeavours. However, in pursuit of all these attributes, in a very subtle manner I became somewhat of a perfectionist; almost veering towards the proverbial my way or the highway kind of attitude. In the early stages of my professional life, I was driven by an obsessive desire to succeed which in many respects engendered undue pressure on me. These perceived successes started to become a matter of routine yet left me quite hollow and even widened the distance between me and others. We all have a desire to be in control because control gives us a sense of certainty. As I moved on in in life, I discovered that certainty is an illusion. There are quite a few things in life that we simply have no control over.

I am sure that at some stage of your life you also got sucked into this vicious cycle. What was the key that delivered me from the above set of circumstances? I had to embrace the principle of surrender. The word surrender has initially been a big struggle for me, and I am in a continuous process of maturing in this regard. It brought me to the realisation that I do not always have to be in charge of something, know all the causative factors about everything that's happening in my life, always need to come out tops or go extraordinary lengths to do something in order to be accepted and appreciated. Living a surrendered life was an extremely liberating experience because instead of always hitting cul de sac signs, I started to see new possibilities. Letting go of something should not be seen as a weakness but rather viewed as an innate strength where you do not allow yourself to be consumed by any set of circumstances. Surrender is an immeasurable and transcending power that can ever happen in one's life. It is not a passive denialism of the current reality but having an open and responsive attitude to new possibilities.

For many years in my life and I am sure in your life as well, there has always been this niggling and recurring question – what if? It hits you unannounced and at times least expected yet can be very profound and uncomfortable. Questions such as – what if:

- I lose my job and is not able to afford the current lifestyle my family is enjoying now?
- The results of the biopsy I have done last week suggest that I am having cancer?
- I went for a Covid-19 test today and the results are positive?
- My spouse gets hooked up with one of my best friends and my marriage lands on the rocks?

- The business venture in which I invested so heavily becomes insolvent?
- My teenage daughter who I brought up so well, gets entangled in an abusive relationship?...What if? ...What if?...

These are uncomfortable questions in life that can rob us of our peace and has the potential to completely derail us in pursuit of our destiny. These are the things over which we have most of the times absolutely no control and our only recourse is to embrace the spirit of surrender.

In 1934 Reinhold Niebuhr wrote the following powerful piece that became the Serenity Prayer.

> *"God give me grace to accept with serenity the things that cannot be changed. Courage to change the things which should be changed and the wisdom to distinguish the one from the other. Living one day at a time and enjoying one moment at a time. Accepting hardships as a pathway to peace... Trusting that You will make all things right, if I surrender to Your will. So that I may be reasonably happy in this life and supremely happy with You in the next. Amen."* [62]

In June 2019 I was ministering one Sunday morning at a church in Hartbeespoort. Nobody in the congregation except my wife, knew that I was suffering from a cardiac problem and was due for surgery the next Tuesday. I felt good throughout the whole week but became extremely weak and wobbly whilst preaching. Through God's grace, I managed to soldier on and land my sermon on the right note. The Lord ministered to me in such a unique and special way after the service. A gentleman by the name of Lourens whom I had never met before, walked up to me, and asked whether he can talk to Liz and myself. He told us that whilst I was preaching, three times the Lord revealed to him that I am in need of strength and the Lord will lead me victoriously through whatever is currently wearing me down. I was dumbstruck. This word was spot-on and it carried me through arguably one of the biggest health challenges I had to face in many decades. I successfully underwent surgery and completely recovered.

Living a surrendered life means that I can wholeheartedly trust God for my marriage, children, finances, the future of our country, my health and wellbeing, wisdom to excel in my leadership assignments, just about every facet of my life.

May I ask you to please reflect very seriously on this statement: The area in my life I most need to surrender is.......

Let it go!

I trust that you appreciate by now that you make your decisions, and your decisions make you. To create the best future for our lives, the options are abundantly clear – a qualitative choice or merely going through the motions. You need to take a conscious and deliberate decision that you want to enter the realm of boundless opportunity. A good starting point is to retrace your steps and remind yourself about the times when you were at your best, most passionate, engaged, and effective. Call to remembrance the times you were most at peace and what was happening in the various parts of your life that made you feel that way. It will also be equally important to confront your most painful life experiences in an honest and rational manner; what have you learned from it and the extent that it shaped your current outlook towards life. As you go through the latter, you will have to consciously work on replacing the hurtful memories, setbacks, and failures with an appreciation for who you really are and all the positive attributes that reside in you. Recognize the divine power within you, seize the opportunities around you and move forward to lay hold of your destiny.

After your time of reflecting on the above-mentioned issues, you will be well advised to think through a realistic action plan to regain lost ground and move forward in a focused and decisive manner. It all hinges around the right motives, information, people, resources, results and sacrifices to be made. To ensure that you remain on track, you also need to set up structures of accountability to hold you to your commitment. This might take on the form of a mentor, coach or confidant. Nothing of significance was ever accomplished by anybody without the input, support, and accountability to others. As you progress on your journey, unashamedly celebrate progress and significant milestones. Never neglect an opportunity to affirm those that helped you on your journey. Appreciate and recognize the value and potential of others. In the final analysis, it is all about living a life that reflects the character and nature of your Creator in all your endeavors.

You were born for greatness, to transform your immediate sphere of influence far beyond what you can imagine. This can only be brought about by the quality of your decisions. It is time to come alive and enter the realm of endless possibility. You have one life to live, live it now!

Chapter 13

THE PRECIOUS GIFT OF HEALING AND WHOLENESS

Power dictates what should be spoken about, where and by whom. We are living in a world where a host of distorted power relations are playing itself out in the political, racial, gender and economic spheres to name but a few. Even religious discourses can exert power over some people by other people. It is no secret that the voice of religion has marginalised and hurt many lives. The role of religion in bolstering an abhorrent and totally ungodly system of apartheid in our very own country's unfortunate past, cannot be underscored in this regard.

The society in which we live, is in desperate need of healing and compassion. It is having a sense of being moved by others suffering so that your heart responds to their pain. Compassion is not only about pity, sympathy, and charity. True compassion at its apex, levels the playing field and its final outcome is healing and wholeness. A critical set of questions that beg answers are: "Where does our understanding of God fits into our current reality?" "What is going on in our spiritual world?" "Is the church able to adequately adapt to the various changes, human awakening and consciousness in our day and age?"

Our journey of spiritual formation is inherently personal. For some our spiritual awareness started at a very early age during childhood and for others, the journey might have started much later. Kindly allow me to raise this question with you – what is the foundational faith of your personal world? Put differently – how do you know what you know? Our faith journey is an evolving one and not a big bang event. It is not merely a journey of doing but one of becoming. According to James Fowler *"Faith is not a separate dimension of life, a compartmentalized speciality. Faith is an orientation of the total person, giving purpose and goal to one's hopes and strivings, thoughts and actions."* [63]

My journey of faith started during my childhood days in the Apostolic Faith Mission Church (AFM). The AFM is the oldest Pentecostal church in South Africa and has extraordinarily strong traditions. Rumour has it that as a child to the amusement of others, I would even imitate the fiery preaching style of some of the pastors. Memorising Bible verses was my favourite pastime. The tradition of the church was however very strict, insulated and even judgemental towards other mainline churches. There was at times an exaggerated sin consciousness as opposed to a God consciousness. We were not even allowed to go to the movies or being with crowds watching a soccer game. Our circle of friends was confined to those in the church community because others outside our church domain were regarded as sinners. I have seen at an early stage of my life, how adults who have "sinned" or transgressed church laws were publicly chastised in church services and put under "sensuur" (censorship). Very subtly, I put in a near impossible effort to conform to the norms of the church to feel worthy and gave me a sense of belonging.

As alluded to earlier, my father walked out on us as a family when I was in Standard 8 (Grade 10) and this was quite disruptive in many ways. He was a leader in the church, and this further confused me when this incident happened. The support system from the church in our moment of despair, was very scanty and I increasingly drifted away from the church; never setting my foot in a church for at least 14 years thereafter. My mind was pre-occupied with many unanswered questions for example: "Why must this happen to me at a time when I needed the steady hand of a father figure the most during my turbulent teenage years?" I veered off into all manner of deviant behaviour, started to indulge in alcohol and increasingly becoming hooked on marijuana. I am naturally a greatly confident person but at that stage of my life I suffered from a severe inferiority complex. My mother's faith remained steadfast, and I featured very prominently in her prayer life for a turnaround in my life.

I went back to the AFM in 1982 and attended church for a few weeks with a hidden agenda. It was merely about my firstborn to be dedicated to the Lord in the church because that is how we were brought up. Surprisingly after the dedication of my daughter Esther, we continued to attend. I found the situation quite different in church than when I left 14 years prior and felt increasingly at home. On the night of the 9 October 1982, a sermon was preached in that church and towards the end the preacher extended an invitation to those who knew that their lives were not in the right relationship with God, to come back home. I still cannot explain what happened to me, but there was just this intense inner conviction in my heart that this invitation was for me. I walked to the front, someone prayed for me and afterwards I just prayed a simple prayer of repentance. My life has never been the same after that. I turned my back on my old lifestyle, submitted myself to a process of discipleship and the results were evident in my life. I increasingly started to live out my faith in the workplace and became actively involved in the Hospital Christian Fellowship. I served as the organisation's General Secretary for ten years in the then Transvaal.

Old attitudes die hard and so while I was ascending into the position of youth leader as well as a member of the Church Board, there was a resurgence of some of the traditional stances that previously characterised the church. Instead of preaching the Gospel, we were subjected to long and sometimes out of context teachings about why women should wear hats, no make-up and earrings, formal dress code for men, overly critical about contemporary gospel music and just so many other non-essentials informed by the traditions of men clothed in all manner of religious jargon. After being in continuous conflict with the leadership and questioning the Scriptural basis for their hard-line attitudes I left the church in an amicable manner. What I tried to avoid, is that my continuous presence must become a source of strife.

After visiting quite a few churches in town, our family opted for Word of Life Church in 1987 which was based in a suburb in the centre of town. It was a small yet intimate set-up. We were the first Black family to officially become members of the church and in those days, it was such a rare thing. We had strong pastoral support by two very dedicated people, Andre and Helena De Kock and the congregation started to experience commendable growth. One of the assistant pastors was the late Brian Winkler, an exceptional teacher of the Word. He circulated a questionnaire amongst all members of the congregation on Spiritual Gifts. At the end of the process, he approached me with the results wherein it was indicated that the two of us were the only two in the congregation which the results shown had strong teaching gifts. He undertook to mentor me and walked a very interactive journey with me. It is so comforting to know when somebody believes in you, and this is what I experienced with Brian. I am highly indebted to him for recognising the gift in me that the Lord graced me with and mentored me in this regard. We made quite a few solid friends across the racial divide amongst the congregants and there was a genuine and sincere sense of community.

Under Helena's leadership, the church branched out into Christian schooling. The Klerksdorp Christian Academy was established with a strong multiracial focus and educational excellence. On the 16th of December 1991 at about 01h30 in the morning, tragedy hit our church. Our auditorium and some of the newly built educational infrastructure on site were bombed down. There was a militant Right Wing White Supremacist group called the Afrikaner Weerstand Beweging (AWB) operative in our part of the country that claimed responsibility for it. In the history of the Afrikaner, the 16th of December by then, was an incredibly significant day and it was called the Day of the Covenant. It has its roots in the Battle of Blood River on 16 December 1838. The besieged Voortrekkers took a public vow before the battle. In return for God's help in obtaining victory over the Zulus, they promised to build a church and forever honour this day as a holy day of God. They won a bloody battle, and this vow was honoured. Regrettably, it also informed their White supremacist perspective for many decades to follow. This act of the AWB, was an extraordinary expression of honoring that covenant. The only sin of the people of Word of Life was to have an open church community as opposed to the segregated churches based on racial lines. An extension of this was to give equal education opportunities to every deserving child regardless of race or class, with a strong Christian foundation. Where does Blood River features in this noble initiative? This was diabolical to their view of Christianity, and they had the nerve to spray graffiti on the walls in which they indicated that it was done in remembrance of the covenant.

This was also the time when there was a lot of political fluidity in the country with the release of Nelson Mandela and the unbanning of political organisations. As I stood near the rubble that day of what remained of our sanctuary, I had a lot of such mixed emotions. Why this hatred and level of destruction? Where is God in all these things? How long is this level of misplaced White domination going to continue? To say that our congregation was devastated, is an understatement. Andre and Helena tried to keep the church going as we moved from house to house every week having our services. The numbers were dwindling drastically especially some of the businesspeople who feared that their businesses would be adversely affected by being associated with Word of Life. During that time, right wing terror reigned supreme in our part of the world. Word of Life ultimately closed as a church but out of the rubble, the site has been developed into a very successful educational centre and Klerksdorp Christian Academy became a school of note in the North West Province.

We then out of necessity moved to Rhema Church - Orkney in 1992. Once we settled in at Rhema, I fell again into the trap of being critical and judgemental about the old-style Pentecostal churches and developed almost a misplaced spiritual superiority of being part of the charismatic movement. I was however rudely awakened to discover that amidst the happy clappy atmosphere, Rhema church's sense for social justice was non-existent by then.

The congregation in Orkney at that time, consisted of only about 7% Black members. It usually struck me how they could sing songs like – This is our land, this is our nation. At the height of unrests in Black townships in the early 90's, there would be words of "prophesy" spoken over the congregation about no weapon formed against them shall prosper. It almost appeared to me that God took sides in favour of those that were benefitting from an unjust system and there was no message of hope for those of us labouring under the constraints of apartheid. A power discourse where the defence of unfair privilege is now Biblically justified, caused me to seriously reflect on what the God of the Bible said about the then social context we found ourselves in. I discovered that contrary to the subtle narrative propagated in my church, the Bible declared in Isaiah 1 :17 (NIV) "*Learn to do right; seek justice. Defend the oppressed. Take up the cause of the fatherless; plead the case of the widow.*" In Isaiah 10 :1 – 2 (NIV) "*Woe to those who make unjust laws, to those who issue oppressive decrees to deprive the poor of their rights and withhold justice from the oppressed of my people...*"

Without being judgemental and with absolute sincere motives, I engaged Pastor Tim Salmon. I was surprised about his open and responsive attitude. One could almost sense a relief from his side that someone broke the ice. He opened up space for highly interactive group discussions off site, on how to construct a more inclusive church environment and deal with unconscious bias. I also made a concerted effort to reach out across the racial divide and very strong friendships were fostered. It was also the time after the Kairos Conference in Rustenburg where church leaders like Beyers Naude, Desmond Tutu, Peter Storey, Frank Chikane, Johann Heyns and Ray McCauley charted a new vision on how the church must play its role in normalising society. The efforts of these church leaders made an indelible impression on me.

In 1994 when I entered the political arena as MEC of Finance in the North West Province, it did not come without controversy. My Pentecostal colleagues in Alabama doubted whether I was still a believer because the ANC in their discourse, was regarded as communists and ungodly. When my pastor announced about my intentions to avail myself for political office and that he is supportive of my decision, he was viewed with great suspicion amongst the congregants. Not long after I relocated to Mafikeng, Pastor Tim Salmon merely made a remark during a sermon about the enriching experience he had after reading the book Long Walk to Freedom by Nelson Mandela. Consequently, eight families resigned from the church after that remark.

We were fortunate when I relocated to Mafikeng that there was a Rhema branch there. For ten years we fellowshipped at Rhema New Life Church under the able stewardship of Pastor Mike and Michelle Tessendorf. The pastoral care we received during the challenging times of a high-profile political life, kept us grounded as a family. Pastor Mike also did not shy away from visiting me at times to confront me pastorally in areas where he noticed I was veering off course. I really valued that level of accountability.

During my political tenure and afterwards when I entered the corporate world, I had so many beautiful experiences in my interactions with people of other persuasions in the broader Christian community and engage with them through the eyes of God's love. My life has been so enriched by gaining new perspectives and insights about the various symbols, liturgy, styles of worship and the various mediums through which the Good News gets communicated.

As I progressed in my journey of faith, I developed a much healthier appreciation for my spiritual roots in the AFM. My greatest respect goes to the many men and woman of God who might not always have had it theologically correct, but still out of genuine and sincere considerations imparted certain values into my life to enrich my journey of faith. I am in regular contact with some of the leaders in the AFM church and occasionally ministered in some of their congregations. They have definitely come a long way in shifting the dial on some of their rigid practices and unwarranted power discourses for which I am grateful.

As for the blow inflicted on my spiritual journey at Word of Life, this spurred me on to make my contribution in bringing about a just society as God envisaged. It brought me to the realisation that God cannot be commoditised for our own parochial ambitions. With my children still at a tender age then, I had to take decisive responsibility for the ministry of reconciliation entrusted unto us, so that they would not have to face the cruelties of an ungodly system that I had to endure as a child.

Concerning the disillusionment I experienced about the lack of a sense of social justice when I joined the Rhema Church in Orkney, I can honestly say that it actually strengthened my resolve in making a small contribution towards social cohesion in our country. I could easily have walked away, but it was in the crucible of an abnormal society that I had to learn what real community should be like, especially among my Christian brothers from different racial and social backgrounds. This was such an important training ground that prepared me for some of the major leadership assignments that God had planned for me.

According to John Chrysostom *"This is the rule of the most perfect Christianity, its most exact definition, its highest point, namely, the seeking of the common good... for nothing can so make a person an imitator of* Christ *as caring for his neighbours"* [64] I can confidently say that we have come a long way in my spiritual home at Rhema Church where I am now fellowshipping at the Randburg congregation for the last 17 years. We are one of the most integrated communities of faith in the Gauteng province with a very strong vision built on the following four pillars - spiritually vibrant, socially significant, evangelically potent and prophetically relevant. This vision is impacting thousands of lives daily. I have great respect for my Pastor Ray McCauley, who took the plunge in the heydays of apartheid to Mastermind what the Master had in Mind and built a multiracial church when it was not the norm by then. He plays a leading role in shaping the moral conscience of our country and unity of purpose in the wider church community. I had the privilege to serve in our church's Financial Advisory Board for seven years and am currently in the leadership of the Band of Brothers and very active in Partners 4 Life, the church's marital support group.

Since 2016, I have been serving on the Board of Coram Deo and has been appointed as Chairperson in February 2021. It is a major counselling centre started by the Dutch Reformed Church - Oosterlig where hundreds of people are being helped annually. This assisted me greatly in developing my conjunctive faith. I even completed the two- year Advanced Programme in Narrative Pastoral Counselling through the University of Pretoria - cum laude in 2019. My involvement at Coram Deo gave me exposure to a part of the faith community that responds to a world beset by all manner of intense trauma, hurts, addictions and pain. My own paradigms were challenged on many aspects. It brought me to the realisation that there are certain realities for which we do not have rigid theological answers.

In moments like these, our only recourse is love, empathy and support as Jesus would have done. I came to the realisation that I was made for more than just been stuck in a theological box that is of no effect to those in my immediate sphere of influence.

I would like to now deal with an extremely sensitive aspect of my life in which I really experienced total healing and restoration. As indicated earlier, my dad was not part of my life for at least 25 years. There were times when I became aware of his whereabouts and tried to reach out to him without success. Just before I left Mafikeng, we established a firm sense of connectedness, our contact was more frequently and when I settled in Hartbeespoort, we were really in regular contact and genuinely being part of each other's lives again. I can say without a shadow of doubt, that we grew very close. I really enjoyed the catchup sessions and what I really miss quite often is when we held hands in prayer before we departed from his place in Eldorado Park and his characteristic pronouncement of blessing over me. He became one of my biggest cheer leaders and always encouraged me in the things of the Lord. He had a deep admiration for Liz and the two of them were also very close.

There is one incident, I will never forget. On Father's Day in 2014, I ministered at the PPC Church in Eldorado Park. I alerted my dad during the week that I will pop in after church to take him out for lunch. I was pleasantly surprised when I ascended the stage to congratulate the fathers, to see him also in that church; nicely dressed in a black suit, white shirt and red tie. It was the first time that I had the privilege to be with him in church on a Father's Day for many years and I could not help but to ask him to rise as I publicly expressed my gratitude for him being my father. After lunch when I dropped him at home, he held my hands, looked me in the eyes and commended me for delivering a very good sermon on fatherhood. He said to me, I have listened to you now on several occasions and I want to tell you my son that you are an excellent teacher of the Word of God. Excel in this gift and do not try to be anything else. I cannot describe to you the feeling as I listened to him; it really touched my heart. For so many years in my life, I missed the affirmation of my father. His comments that day were so profound and carried with it such meaning; I will never forget that moment.

Towards September 2017, my dad became critically ill with prostate cancer. He was in and out of hospital and the last time he was admitted, I went to see his doctor early one morning at Baragwanath Hospital during the ward rounds. The doctor told me that there was nothing else they could do for him because his illness was terminal and the best we could do, was to take him home and take care of him. The doctor said: "*Mr Kuscus it might be days, weeks or maybe a few months.*" I thank the Lord that He granted us an additional 15 months with my dad, and we even had the privilege of spending time with him on his 87th birthday. On the 23 December 2018 whilst visiting my eldest daughter and her family in Melbourne - Australia, I got a call that dad had passed away.

Jogging my memory, I recalled the almost 25 years when he was not part of my life. This instinctively left me with a few unanswered questions. I can however thank the Lord that for the last 17 years of my dad's life, God miraculously intervened and we became very close to one another. There were no regrets, and I was able to experience God's grace, healing and wholeness in our relationship. It was so befitting for his send off to have taken place in the AFM Church in Eldorado Park. I look forward to seeing him on the other side.

My journey of faith was not merely something to stimulate my intellect or me choosing to embark on a journey of unsubstantiated optimism. It was the development of a personal relationship with my Creator over many years of discovery, contradictions and at times dead-ends in areas for which I simply had no answers. It is this attitude of being open, honest, objective yet responsive on matters of faith, that was arguably the most important aspect of my life that kept me on course in my quest towards living a life of credibility.

I cannot recall any stage of my life where I never believed in God. My journey of faith was however informed by very powerful discourses that at times gave rise to inconsistency in my spiritual development; erratic at best and non-existent at worst. Through all these experiences, there was always this healthy anxiety within me that drove me "You are made for more." Through God's grace, my journey of faith shifted from trying to understand God, to learning to know Him. In my pursuit of having a personal relationship with Him, I do not always have to understand all the granular details, but have absolute trust in Him that He always have my best interest at heart. This desire is so aptly echoed in the words of Paul in Philippians 3:10 (MSG) *"I gave up all the inferior stuff so that I could know Christ personally..."*

This personal and intimate knowledge of Him as I approach each day, brought healing and wholeness into my life. I experience this sense of wholeness as a process of increasingly being at peace and harmony with myself, the environment in which I operate and virtually every facet of my life. I now view the world through the eyes of His love and did not allow any bitterness to inform my current reality. I thank God that I am saved for His glory, healed for His honour, and forgiven for His praise!

Chapter 14

WHAT WILL INFORM THE NEXT CHAPTER IN YOUR BOOK?

Since my early primary school days, I was always an avid reader with an unquenching thirst for knowledge. Going to the library at least twice a week, was an absolute must. Paging those days through the Encyclopaedia Britannica, was a window to a much bigger world that made me feel very learned among my friends. Those were the days when there was no television station in South Africa and reading intriguing novels of authors like Agatha Christie, Heinz Konsalik, James Hadley Chase, Enid Blyton and Wilbur Smith, fed our fertile imaginations.

There is an explosion of knowledge in our day and age. What took me hours to access in a library in my primary school days, can now be available on my mobile phone at the press of a button. The importance for leaders to remain conversant with current information cannot be overemphasised. Lawyers must continually read into case law, doctors on clinical research papers; this keeps them relevant and agile in their respective professional field. Books will always remain a primary source of reference. Circumstances might have changed but there are timeless writings; the truths expressed are still very much relevant for our times and give a tested perspective. It is every writer's dream that his or her book will reach as wide an audience as possible and even achieve best-seller status. The prestige of becoming a best-selling author, accords you great influence and the potential to amass a loyal following.

Our lives are like writing a book. The pages of the book are the sum total of all our endeavours, whether positive or negative and an accurate record of all our thoughts, intentions and actions. Unlike writing a novel, where the narrative is meticulously planned and constructed, the challenge with writing the book of our life, is that we cannot predetermine when the storyline will end.

Phil Cooke in a book titled "One Big Thing" [65] wrote, and I fully concur with his view, that what distinguishes the ordinary person from the extra ordinary ones, is the ability to timeously discover the purpose of their lives. They have a noticeably clear understanding of what they were born to do. Everything they do or intend doing, goes instinctively through the filter of their overarching purpose. Do you really understand what you were born for?

In 2 Corinthians 6: 12 – 13 (MSG) Paul reminds us "*...Your lives are not small, but you're living them in a small way...Open up your lives. Live openly and expansively.*" Opening our lives is an earnest call to look beyond ourselves and our current reality with an eternal legacy in mind. This legacy is written minute by minute, day by day. What is it that you would like to be remembered for? Owned the biggest house in town? Always threw the best parties with all the A-listed celebrities in attendance? Made tons of money? Mover and a shaker that always made headlines...?

The best legacy we can leave behind is a living legacy. You see, material considerations and stuff will go out of fashion and over time loses its lustre and appeal. Investing in people will have an enduring effect. Someone once said – you can see the seeds in an orange, but you cannot see the oranges in the seed. When your legacy is primarily informed by bringing about a change in people's lives, it will definitely have a generational impact.

It is in this context that we must do all we can in ensuring that we build the necessary intergenerational equity for generations to follow. The United Nations (UN) [66], in its report entitled: Intergenerational Solidarity and the needs of future generations, defined the principle as follows: "In broad terms, the pursuit of welfare by the current generation should not diminish the opportunities for a good and decent life for succeeding generations. Thus, concern for the needs of future generations falls into the category of what is sometimes termed intergenerational equity or intergenerational justice, essentially the allocation of the burdens and benefits across generations." (United Nations, 2013).

Today the Intergenerational Equity Principle has emerged as a driving force behind this generation's response to the worsening environmental, social, and economic outlook for the planet and our civilisation. Its principles and ethos have permeated boardrooms, classrooms and occupied the minds of leaders across society and the globe towards the realisation of a more sustainable, just, and prosperous future for generations to come.

I am intensely conscious at this stage of my life about matters of legacy and the decisions that will inform my legacy. It is my fervent desire to pursue those things that matter to the next generation with excellence, a sense of purpose and motivated by nothing other than love. We owe it to future generations to prepare them timeously to take on higher levels of responsibility. We also owe it to the next generation, to leave the global village in a better state we found it in. But above all, we owe it to those who come after us to connect them to a meaningful relationship with God. In so doing, we must conduct ourselves in such a manner to debunk any perceptions about hypocrisy, lack of love and our perceived ignorance about the culture shifts that the younger generation sometimes offer as reasons for their disenchantment about matters of faith.

Imagine it is your 80th birthday and your spouse has planned a quiet evening for just the two of you at your favourite restaurant. When you arrive at the restaurant, you are surprised to see that the whole building has been reserved for you. There are 100 of your closest family, friends, and colleagues there. Then one-by-one, each attendee come up to the microphone in front of the room and speaks to the three issues below.

1. Here is what I admire about you....
2. Here is the difference you made in my life....
3. Your Number One achievement of significance is....

What would you hope them saying?

One of my all-time favourites is a book by Steven Covey – The Seven Habits of Highly Effective People. In habit Number Two he reminds us to always begin with the end in mind. It means, to reach your maximum potential and leave an enduring legacy, one needs to have a compelling picture of what that preferred future should look like. This then becomes the template against which all your endeavours are calibrated. I need to invest daily in what I want to hear on my 80th birthday. It is like operating a bank account, you cannot make a withdrawal (never mind gaining interest) if you do not regularly deposit money into it.

There are three primary seasons in life: struggle, success, and significance. Our early years are filled with the struggle of getting a good education and landing our first job. Our twenties to mid-forties are often filled with the pursuit of success. Once we begin to achieve some level of success, we develop a healthy anxiety because success does not fill our deepest longings. It compels us to search for something much deeper, meaningful, and enduring. In my understanding, this desire is called significance. Regrettably, as I observed what is happening around me, I can confidently say that not everybody transitions from struggle to success and even less people transition from success to significance.

Every person is thinking differently about success. Some people might define success as having luxurious cars and a huge mansion, the ability to travel to exotic destinations and just having fun, carrying a big title in society and have everybody at your beck and call and forever making the social pages in the mainstream media. Others might consider having access to the basic things in life and living a life full of joy and happiness with their family as the true meaning of success. Success is a powerful motivator. It can dictate how we spend our time, energy, and resources. It can influence relationships, schedules, and families. It may even become an all-consuming passion that leaves broken people and morality in its wake. Yet, success is not the highest calling that we have. We have been created to live lives of significance. What do I mean with significance? It is consciously making a positive and impactful difference in the lives of others.

Consider these differences between success and significance:

- Success is like a sand dune in the dessert, it comes and goes. Significance always lasts.
- Success ends on the day you die. Significance carries on long after you departed from the earth.
- Success is never enough and there is always the desire for more. Significance satisfies, brings contentment and is fulfilling.

The foremost question that should pre-occupy our minds when we go to bed every night is, "Whose life did I touch today?" Just like the author who intends writing a book makes a decision about what needs to be communicated; leaving a living legacy starts with a conscious decision about what value would you like to bequeath to the people in your sphere of influence. We must however go beyond the decision; it should be approached with extreme diligence on a consistent basis. The quality of your life is not a function of chance, but by consciously putting yourself in the picture of significance and intentionally pursue it.

Getting back to the 80th birthday party; I personally would very much like to hear the following responses:

1. Here's what I admire about you: You walked in humility and being an embodiment of absolute integrity.
2. Here's the difference you made in my life: You saw the potential in me and was never too busy to create time and opportunity to develop me and impart something positive into my life.
3. Your number One achievement of significance is: Your marriage to Liz for the last 54 years was an example of true love worth emulating. We sincerely appreciate that you are still faithfully serving the younger generation for Kingdom impact.

God willing, one day when you reach 80 years and have the privilege to be showered with such positive accolades at your birthday party, it will be an affirmation of a life well lived. It will not only glorify God but really inspire others. This will not simply happen out of the blue; you must relentlessly work at it. We have but one life to live, let us live each day to His glory in pursuit of significance.

I trust that as each one of us is busy crafting our biography, that when we are not on earth anymore, there will be no missing pages in our book or that the storyline is so incoherent that no one can figure out what your life was all about. Let it rather be said of your book that this is a true reflection of clarity of purpose, utmost faithfulness, derived deeper satisfaction pursuing servanthood and lived an open and expansive life that positively impacted his / her generation.

Start writing that chapter today!

The question raised in Chapter One remains: "Who raises the village?" This question is informed by the following considerations - Who are the voices that shape the thinking, behaviour, and value system of our world? Who are those amongst us whose good judgement can be trusted as we grapple with ever-increasing socio economic challenges confronting our world? Who are the custodians of the ethos that defines our humanity? Who are those amongst us whose credibility is beyond reproach?

God's original intent has always been to have His glory manifested in all facets of our daily lives. Amidst these major culture shifts and socio – economic challenges we dealt with earlier, the necessity for the manifestation of God's glory is even becoming more pronounced in our village. There are three possible ways in which we can respond to some of the daunting challenges:

- Escape into your holy huddle, avoiding any real contact with the real issues in your world and the people affected by it.
- Acculturate and blend in with the environment where compromise reigns supreme without openly declaring where you stand on matters of principle. The downside of this approach is that if you stand for nothing, you will fall for everything.
- Actively engage with the culture of the day and intentionally promote what the appropriate alternative is all about; based on sound convictions and lived out with a high degree of compassion.

With all threats, also come opportunities. The speed at which information can be disseminated and the massive movement of people around the globe today, provide us with countless opportunities from which we can leverage for maximum Kingdom impact. This will warrant that we always have a sense of awareness of what is happening in our village and the implications thereof on its well-being. Trust God for guidance on what you need to commit to in terms of time, talent and even treasure in making a difference. You do not need to carry the burden completely on your own; partner with like- minded people beyond your institutional boundaries, together we can do so much more.

Over the preceding chapters of this book, I have made an attempt to shed some light on the prevailing crisis in leadership in our global village. I came to the conclusion that it is inherently a crisis of credibility. Our leaders on many fronts are no more trusted, believed, admired, and respected. I also attempted to advance some principles on how to regain lost ground on the credibility front and shared some of my own life experiences in this regard. By this, I do not want to propagate it as conclusive but as a basis to start engaging on a journey to appropriately respond to the prevailing leadership crisis. My journey came not without its own imperfections and contradictions, but it was life changing and translated into tremendous fulfilment and impact. I will however be the first to admit that there is still so much more to be done.

Never lose sight of the fact that we are representing a peculiar brand in this world. To be truthful to our origins, commitments, and intentions, requires credible living. The implications for unauthentic and fake living can have serious consequences. *"Let me tell you why you are here. You're here to be salt-seasoning that brings out the God-flavors of this earth. If you lose your saltiness, how will people taste godliness? You've lost your usefulness and will end up in the garbage."* Mathew 5:13 (MSG). Salt is distinctive, penetrative, preserves, flavours, and provokes thirst. It is my fervent desire that as Christian leaders in the marketplace, we shall become a living embodiment of this brand proposition. We have a message worth conveying to the world, let us communicate it in a credible manner. We should never lose our saltiness (credibility) because we will lose our usefulness. If we pursue credibility in every facet of our lives, we will be believed, trusted, admired, and respected for Kingdom impact.

Since you are human, the temptation might be to externalise the changes you would like to see happening in the world in which you find yourself. One of the biggest challenges that all leaders must face, is how ready are you for change in your own personal life. Ron Edminson puts it this way *"Often you have to change yourself before you can encourage change in others. All change starts with one step. The change you are most afraid of is possibly the change you need the most."*[67]

Are you ready to make that change? Are you ready to start with that one step? In our moments of despair and disillusionment, just remember one indisputable fact; God is the final arbiter in the destiny of humanity. Become part of the mighty transformative work that He is doing right now, in our day and age. Be the voice that shapes the value system of our world. I am convinced that if we apply our collective ingenuity, we can turn the tide around for the better. The village is desperately crying out for credible leadership. Will the leader in you show up?

Leaders need to be mindful of the implications their actions and decisions might have on generations to come. At this stage of my life, I want to devote all my energy in pursuing those things that will leave an indelible mark and worth emulating. Our generation needs to ensure that when we exit the scene, we leave our world in a much better shape than how we found it. If you really want to live a life of significance that glorifies God and positively impact on the lives of others, then credibility matters.

Learn it. Live it. Lead it!

Acknowledgements

The famous adage goes: "It takes a village to raise a child." There are countless people that positively impacted on my leadership journey and for that, I will always be grateful. This book is the culmination of the collective effort of quite a few people that made its publication possible. Please allow me to express my special gratitude to:

1. My dear wife Liz and children – Esther, Ezra and Zoe. Thanks for the love, support and respect you accord me to excel in the things God called me to do.
2. Pastor Ray McCauley, my spiritual leader for the last 17 years. You are indeed an embodiment of servanthood which I always endeavour to emulate. Thanks for your words of affirmation; it is much appreciated.
3. My friend Frank Thomas, for a very thought-provoking Foreword. Your razor-sharp intellect never fails to amaze me, yet you always succeed to get your message across in such a graceful manner.
4. Alvin Fredericks my editor; your professionalism was outstanding and greatly assisted to keep me on course. You did an excellent job to refine my thoughts and smoothen the rough edges into a beautiful and cohesive storyline.
5. Samuel Ogbu, Rich Cummins, Snowy Khoza, Steven French, Serge Solomons, Watson Ladzani, Mathilda Fourie, Maurice Radebe, Christa De Wet and Malungelo Zilimbola who wrote such inspiring notes of endorsement. Thanks for taking the time to go through the manuscript and express your opinions about the contents with such honesty and grace.

6. Barry Morkel, Sol Motsepe, Dumani Kula, Antoinette Prophy, Sam Alexander, David Molapo and Madeline Lass. These are friends whose expertise I value and hence my request to them to critique the manuscript. Your inputs were invaluable in enriching the final output of this book.
7. The team at Westbow publishers for holding my hand in ensuring that we have an excellent product to present to the readers.
8. Last but not least, my Heavenly Father who faithfully carried me through the various life experiences that I had to go through. It is through Your grace that I am still standing. My utmost desire is to live a life of credibility that will be pleasing to You.

References

Introduction

1 Transparency International, *2020 Global Corruption Perception Index*, 28 January 2021

2 Transparency International, *Five Cases of Trouble at the Top*, 28 January 2021.

Chapter 1.

3 WEF Article in collaboration with Visual Capitalist,*70 Years of urban growth in infographics*, 3 September 2019.

4 Statista, *Total Population Worldwide 2019*, Published by Aaron O'Neil, 1 April 2021.

5 Oxfam International Report, *World's Billionaires have more Wealth than 4,6 billion people*, 20 January 2020.

6 John Maxwell, *Leadership Gold*, (Thomas Nelson, Nashville, 2008) 68 -69

7 David Mc Kenna – *Never Blink in a Hailstorm*, (Baker Books, Grand Rapids Michigan, 2005) 29 -33

8 Masters Thesis of Oluoch Otiena, *The Christian Political Theory of Rt. Rev. Dr. Henry Okullu*, University of Kwazulu Natal 2003.

9 Phyllis Hendry, *Lead Like Jesus Summit*, Acts Church, Midrand, South Africa, 26 July 2016

10 Article in Brad A Cox Website – *If You Can't Mess up, don't bother leading.*

11 Desmond Tutu, *10 Pieces of Wisdom from Desmond Tutu on his Birthday*, Desmond Tutu Peace Foundation, 7 October 2015.

12 Chip Conley – *Wisdom at Work* (Penguin Random House UK, 2018) 15-23

Chapter 3.

13 Article by Maurilio Amorim, *Building and Protecting your Personal Brand*, Church Leaders Website, 8 August 2011

14 Hal Seed, *3 Unspoken Promises People Expect Leaders to Keep*, Sermon Central, 7 March 2020

Chapter 4.

15 David Stoddard, *The Heart of Mentoring*, (Nav Press, Colorado Springs,1953) 141-142
16 Jon Bloom, *Wake up to the Corrupting Effects of Compromise*, designingGod.org 27 July 2015.
17 Blog from the Billy Graham Library, *10 Quotes from Billy Graham* on Money, 3 June 2020
18 Hillgert, Truesdell and Lochhaas, *Christian Ethics in the Workplace*, (Concordia 2002)
19 Gordon Mc Donald, *When Men Think Private Thoughts*, (Thomas Nelson, Nashville, Tennessee 1997) 98
20 Gordon Mc Donald, *A Resilient Life*, (Nelson Books, Nashville, Tennessee,2004) 143 -146
21 Gustavo Razetti, *Watch your Thoughts for they become Destiny*, Article in Fearless Culture Design, 4 January 2019

Chapter 5.

22 Kevin Paul Scott, *Sight without Vision*. Blog on kevinpaulscott.com March 2020.
23 Sermon quotation archive, *Pastoral Resources*, studylight.org
24 Odufuwa Olusegun Blog 23 August 2016
25 Marshall Segal, *The Lethal Drug in your Dream Job*, designingGod.com 16 October 2014
26 David Mc Kenna, *Never Blink in a Hailstorm*, (Baker Books, Grand Rapids Michigan, 2005) 35 -39
27 Martin Gover, *The Simplest Book Ever on Life, Attitude and Happiness*, (Kindle unlimited, November 2012)
28 Bob Buford, *Half Time*, (Zondervan, Grand Rapids, Michigan 1994) 83 – 89

Chapter 6.

29 Dan Markovitz, *The Signature of Mediocrity is Chronic Inconsistency*, Article in Markovitz Consulting 25 September 2012.
30 Dawkins Brown, *Excellence is Never an Accident*, Linkedin 30 December 2017
31 David Stoddard, *The Heart of Mentoring*, (NavPress, Colorado Springs 1953) 77
32 Jim Collins, *First Who, Then What, Article in Concepts* by Jim Collins 2021.
33 Marvin J. Ashton, Daily Dependence, Daily Devotions by Marvin Ashton, 18 May 2020.
34 Tony Dungy, *The Mentor Leader*, (Tyndale House, Carol Stream Illinois, 2010) 22- 23
35 Myles Munroe, *Passing it On*, Faith Words, May 2011.

Chapter 7.

36 Larry Osborne, Article published in Christianity Today 19 May 2004
37 Bill Donahue, *The ABC of Deep Personal Change*, Church leaders blog
38 Steve Meuller, *Ralph Emmerson Waldo Quotes*, www.planetofsuccess.com 24 January 2020
39 Mark Zuckerberg, Facebook Post 31 July 2015
40 Rose Pastere, *Fast Company*, 1 December 2015

Chapter 8.

41 David Lee, *Make Network Marketing Work* (Google Books 2006)
42 Mike Myatt, *Forbes Magazine*, 9 February 2012.
43 Larry Crabb, *Inside Out* (Google Books 2007)

Chapter 9.

44 Carol Harper, *Article in Pain Pathways Magazine*, 10 October 2015.
45 Oswald Saunders, *Spiritual Leadership* (Moody Publishers, Chicago 2007) 71- 72, 156 -157
46 Carrol Mann, *The 19th Hole: Favourite Golf Stories* (Longmeadow Publishers, 1992)
47 Bradley, *Abey and Ford, How Much is Enough?* (Zebra Press, Cape Town, 2015) 190 -191
48 Oswald Saunders, *Spiritual Leadership* (Moody Publishers, Chicago 2007) 71- 72, 156 -157
49 Optimize, *Quotes on action Modern Classic* – Optimize Enterprises 2021.
50 Quote Master – quotemaster.org 2021
51 Marilyn Carlson Nelson, *How we lead Matters* (Mc Graw Hill, New York 2008)
52 Executive Leader Podcast – *3 Questions Every Follower is asking about their leader*, The John Maxwell Co. 15 May 2018.
53 Gracious Quotes, *62 Wise Thomas Fuller Quotes*, 12 February 2020
54 Sunday Mancini, *Three Lessons from Chimanda Adichie's – The Danger of a* Single *Story*, Ethos 3, 11 April 2016.
55 Brene Brown, *Braving the Wilderness: The Quest for True Belonging and the Courage to Stand Alone* (Random House, New York, 2017)
56 Rick Warren, *How to Fight Against the Three Fears*, Purpose Driven Church Blog, 20 November 2018.
57 Scott Sauls, *Cultivating Iron- Sharpens – Iron Friendships in the Church, Church Leaders*, 8 February 2017.
58 John Bunyan, CoolNsmart.com 2006
59 UN Department of Economic and Social Affairs News Report, New York, 17 September 2019.

60 David Murray, *The Most Essential Life Skill – Teachability*, Head, Heart and Home, 4 December 2015.

Chapter 12.

61 Leonard Ravenhill, Goodreads Quotes

Chapter 13.

62 Trevor Hudson, *The Serenity Prayer* (Upper Room Books, Nashville 2012)

Chapter 10.

63 James Fowler, *Stages of Faith,* (Harper One, New York, 1981) 3- 14

64 Jim Wallis, *(Un) Common Good* (Brazos Press, Grand Rapids Michigan, 2014) 3

Chapter 14.

65 Phil Cooke, *One Big Thing,* (Thomas Nelson, Nashville 2012)

66 United Nations, *Intergenerational Solidarity and the needs of future generations,* United Nations 2013

67 Ron Edminson, *12 Random Thoughts on Change*, Church Leaders – Pastor Blogs.

About the Author

Martin Kuscus is a well-known business leader from South Africa. Over the last 35 years, he distinguished himself in quite a few high-profile positions that he occupied in government as well as the corporate world both local and internationally. He was the first MEC of Finance in the North West Provincial Government from 1994 until 2004. Prior to that, he spent 17 years in health care services. In June 2004 he became CEO of the South African Bureau of Standards a position he held until July 2009. From 2006 – 2009 he was Chairperson of the Government Employee Pension Fund (GEPF); presiding over a R920 billion portfolio and by then the seventh biggest pension fund in the world. In 2009 after exiting the public sector, he then started his own business ventures. He currently occupies directorships on the boards of companies in the health care, financial services, telecoms and built environment sectors.

As a gifted communicator, he addressed audiences in many countries in conferences and high impact meetings. Given his rich experience and strategic insights, he became a trusted coach and mentor to quite a few influential leaders in the corporate and church environments.

Kindly visit Martin's website martinkuscus.org for additional information and avail yourself of some of his complimentary offerings.

Printed in the United States
by Baker & Taylor Publisher Services